HOW TO WRITE POEMS FOR CHILDREN

ALSO BY
JAMES REEVES

Collected Poems 1929–1959
The Questioning Tiger
Subsong

POEMS FOR CHILDREN

The Wandering Moon
Prefabulous Animiles with Edward Ardizzone
Ragged Robin with Jane Paton
The Blackbird in the Lilac (Oxford University Press)
Jackie Thimble (Chatto & Windus)

ANTHOLOGIES

Heinemann's Junior Poetry Books: a collection of rhymes and poems
for use in primary schools
   1 *Yellow Wheels*
   2 *Grey Goose and Gander*
   3 *Green Broom*
   4 *Strawberry Fair*
The Merry-Go-Round (the above four books in one volume)
Orpheus Book I (English poetry for 10–12-year-olds)
Orpheus Book II (English poetry for 13–15-year-olds)
The Poets' World (an anthology of English Poetry)
The Speaking Oak (a miscellany of English prose and poetry)
A New Canon of English Poetry (with Martin Seymour-Smith)
also: selections in the Poetry Bookshelf Series

ABOUT POETRY

Teaching Poetry
A Short History of English Poetry
The Critical Sense (practical criticism of prose and poetry)
Understanding Poetry
Inside Poetry (with Martin Seymour-Smith)

JAMES REEVES

How to Write Poems
for Children

HEINEMANN

LONDON

Heinemann Educational Books Ltd
LONDON EDINBURGH MELBOURNE TORONTO
SINGAPORE JOHANNESBURG AUCKLAND
IBADAN HONG KONG NAIROBI NEW DELHI

ISBN 0 435 18773 2

Published by
Heinemann Educational Books Ltd
48 Charles Street, London W1X 8AH

Printed in Great Britain
by Butler & Tanner Ltd, Frome and London

Contents

Preface

IN OFFERING this handbook to those interested in the subject, from either a theoretical or a practical standpoint, the last thing I wish to give them is a formal manual of instruction—a *gradus ad Parnassum*, in the seventeenth-century sense. For one thing, I am not competent to write it: for another, it could not be written. Only if there were received ideas of perfection in any art could formal rules be drawn up. Today in the arts anything goes. The proof of the practice is its success in pleasing. In the heyday of classical education everyone knew—or thought he knew—what constituted good verse: it should be in Latin, as like as possible to that of Ovid and Virgil. Hence it was possible, in offering rules for the translation of English into Latin, to draw up lists of epithets, which could be chosen according to how they fitted into the hexametric rhythmic structure. If, on the other hand, you accept certain poems for children by, say, Christina Rossetti, R. L. Stevenson and Walter de la Mare as being among the best of their kind, you could theoretically draw up rules for producing similar results. How useless it would be, and how far short of those standards the results would fall.

No poet, however formal, theoretical and 'objective' his attitude, can usually do much more than describe and illustrate his own procedures. I have no purpose here more than to show how I have written verse for children, as I have over the past twenty-five years. It might have been truer to call this book 'How I Write Poems for Children', but this title seems to me, illogically perhaps, more exhibitionist than the one I have chosen.

Three things are necessary for a writer of children's poems: imagination, technique and taste. Without the first, his work will be pedestrian. It will never, even at its best, become air-borne. Without some technical skill in the handling of language, some knowledge—partly instinctive—of the possibilities and limitations of words and the rhythm and feel of language, his flights of imagination will never remain airborne. The reader will feel let down. Taste is an indefinable faculty, partly negative in its application. It will at least show him what to avoid. It will prevent his playing to the gallery by exploiting the mere passing phases of a child's interests, and help to ensure that what is offered as poetry will be worthy, not only of reading, but of re-reading.

For permission to make the copious quotations from my own verse without which my precepts would be of no value I am indebted to the holders of the copyright, William Heinemann Ltd and the Oxford University Press. A list of all such quotations and their sources will be found at the end of the book.

J. R.

Lewes, 1971

PART I

The Content of Children's Poetry

CHAPTER I

IMAGINATION AND FANTASY

In one of my poems for children occurs the couplet:

> Moths and moonshine mean to me
> Magic—madness—mystery.

This is literally true. Moths, with their mad suicidal obsession, not yet trained out of them by natural selection, have always fascinated me. The moon is archetypally associated with madness. Both moths and moonshine have not yet, so far as I am concerned, yielded all their secrets to science. Nor will they ever do so to the childlike eye. As I write, man has just landed on the moon and found out that it is not made of green cheese. But even now that samples of the moon are in the world's laboratories, the moon has not lost its mystery for the earthly mind. All that was ever said and thought about it is still poetically valid, even though it may be scientifically untrue. After all, we know most of what there is to know about the life-cycle of the moth. Children are taught about it in primary schools. But 'nature study' has not destroyed the study of nature, nor the contemplation of its mysteries. Any child rambling in the country, or even in the allotments and back gardens of a conurbation, can observe with wonder the forms of life that succeed one another in the evolution of the butterfly or moth *imago*: the minute, neat rows of the *ova*, the crawling *larvae* making lace of a neglected cabbage leaf, the dormant *pupa* suspended under a windowsill.

One of the functions of poetry is to preserve, to nourish and to extend the sense of wonder evoked by the natural world. If it is objected that poetry distorts or falsifies nature as understood by science, I can only say that I have never met anyone whose

early interest in poetry has had this result. The scientific en-
thusiast who considers it wicked to teach a child scientific
untruth, such as that the moon is made of green cheese, lacks
a sense of humour and a sense of proportion. The child is not
taken in. He knows it is make-believe: pretence and fantasy
add spice to life. A child without a natural sense of wonder, a
relish for madness, magic and mystery—and I have yet to
meet him—will take no harm from poetry, nor anything else
much. The child with a strong imagination will make up his
own fantasies, whether he reads poetry or not.

But this is mainly an expository book, intended for readers
who do not need to be persuaded of the use of poetry for
children; it is not one of propaganda for those who are sus-
picious of it. If my attitude to poetry is unashamedly romantic,
I can do nothing about it: it is the only one that makes sense
to me. Poetry is not opposed to reason; it is supra-rational. It
is the evidence that there are 'more things in heaven and earth
than are dreamed of in your philosophy'.

> Age after age and all alone,
>   She turns through endless space,
> Showing the watchers on the earth
>   Her round and rocky face.
> Enchantment comes upon all hearts
>   That feel her lonely grace.
>
> Mount Newton is the highest peak
>   Upon the wandering moon,
> And there perhaps the witches dance
>   To some fantastic tune,
> And in the half-light cold and grey
>   Their incantations croon . . .

That is the beginning of the first poem in my first book of
children's verse. It is of course pure fantasy. The poem is based
on beliefs about the moon traditional before the development
of inductive science. It is pure play. It invites the childlike mind

to explore in fantasy a phenomenon too remote (for the present) to explore in actuality.

If there is an easily defined difference between *poetry*—adult poetry—and poetry for children, it is that the former is an exploration of the interior world of the mature mind; the latter is an exploration of the outer world, the world as reported by the senses. I did not feel qualified to write poems for children until I had been writing adult poems for over twenty years. I then felt technically competent, as well as sufficiently assured to know what I was doing. To say one is 'technically competent' is really to say, not that one knows what to do (one is always finding out), but that one knows what not to do. One knows at least how not to write for children: and this is a first step to positive competence. Is it too much to say that, in learning any art or craft, one learns only by one's own mistakes? As a matter of fact, so far as I was concerned, at least at the beginning, my poems for children were technical experiments. But children are too important to be subjected to technical experiments. For them a poem must be something more. I had, as it were, to see that the experiments were successful before offering the results to children. In passing, it may be remarked of those 'modernists' who demand that poetry must be experimental, that what they mean is that poems should be failures: for if in creative work an experiment succeeds, it is no longer an experiment. I shall have much to say later about technique. For the present I am concerned with subject-matter, and in particular the matter of exploration.

Under Ground is an attempt to explore imaginatively a region to which most of us have little access.

> In the deep kingdom under ground
> There is no light and little sound.
>
> Down below the earth's green floor
> The rabbit and the mole explore.
>
> The quarrying ants run to and fro
> To make their populous empires grow.

Do they, as I pass overhead,
Stop in their work to hear my tread?

Some creatures sleep and do not toil,
Secure and warm beneath the soil.

Sometimes a fork or spade intrudes
Upon their earthy solitudes.

Downward the branching tree-roots spread
Into the country of the dead.

Deep down, the buried rocks and stones
Are like the earth's gigantic bones.

In the dark kingdom under ground
How many marvellous things are found!

To say that my view of children's poetry is romantic is not in the least to say that poems written for them should be romantic. On the contrary, if 'romantic' sometimes has the connotation of 'formally shapeless' or 'amorphous and vague in subject-matter', then the kind of poems that should be given to children are more classical in spirit—formally precise, economical and hard in diction and imagery, imaginative excursions represented in an almost matter-of-fact form. What is important is to make the effort of imagination. In *Under Ground* this consists in assembling a number of known facts and expressing them as an intelligible whole. The reader is invited to consider the ground under his feet as a dark, hidden kingdom. Surface phenomena are first considered; then the mind searches deeper down—to the roots of trees, and finally to the unseen rocks far beneath. Thus the ordered act of exploring from the surface downwards is given concrete expression. I admit to a too great concern with tidying up and rounding off poems, and I now think that *Under Ground* (written over twenty years ago) would have been better without the final couplet.

I have sometimes been criticized for an excessive preoccupation with the rural scene, for not catering for the town-bred reader. My reply to this would be twofold. First, I cannot help it. As a poet I am bound to be true to the facts of my experience, and I was brought up almost entirely in the country. To write of the romance of scarlet buses or the bustle of great railway stations or the excitement of a jostling city throng would be, for me, false and forced. I enjoyed cities as a child, but I was always glad to get back to the country again. Life may have pulsated in London, but poetry was in the country. Cities are to me prose. Scarlet buses have a certain rectangular symmetry, but they are noisy and smelly. Railway stations and jostling crowds are noisy and confusing. But there is of course no reason why others should not write poems about these things. An urban poet for children would, however, I think, be one who had been brought up in a city. Then the noise, the smell, the bustle and the movement would be part of his inner world, not a mere distraction from it. He would have to have loved it, not to have wanted to get away from it.

Secondly, children like reading about the country. They enjoy visiting it, and surely nowadays most British children get into the country, if only for too-brief visits. Lastly, I should add that not all of my children's poems are evoked by an exclusively rural setting. Even a child brought up in the heart of a city has seen a line of clothes drying in the wind. He may have no garden, and his view may be bounded by a brick wall, not a hedge; but he has a mental picture of a garden and a hedge.

Stocking and Shirt

Stocking and shirt
    Can trip and prance,
Though nobody's in them
    To make them dance.
See how they waltz
    Or minuet,

Watch the petticoat
  Pirouette.
This is the dance
  Of stocking and shirt,
When the wind puts on
  The white lace skirt.
Old clothes and young clothes
  Dance together,
Twirling and whirling
  In the mad March weather.
'Come!' cries the wind,
  To stocking and shirt.
'Away!' cries the wind
  To blouse and skirt.
Then clothes and wind
  All pull together,
Tugging like mad
  In the mad March weather.

Across the garden
  They suddenly fly
And over the far hedge
  High, high, high!
'Stop!' cries the housewife,
  But all too late,
Her clothes have passed
  The furthest gate.
They are gone for ever
  In the bright blue sky,
And only the handkerchiefs
  Wave good-bye.

In any case, it is not the aim of *this* poem to present a country scene. It is an attempt to evoke the poetic possibilities of something intrinsically commonplace and everyday. If a child has enjoyed a poem in which such things as clothes on a line are made to appear as in a dance, there will always be a trace of poetic possibility in his vision of them in the future. There is indeed nothing *intrinsically* poetic about most things observed in everyday life. It is one function of a writer for children that he can express their poetic possibilities. Poetry is, indeed, largely concerned with possibilities. Emily Dickinson wrote:

> I dwell in possibility,
> A fairer house than prose.

I do not know whether the reading of poetry offers a general training in the envisaging of possibility, but without this kind of imagination what are we planning for? Even the most hard-headed materialist, if his work has any purpose, must have some vision of the end to which he wants us to progress. This may seem a long step from *Stocking and Shirt*, so I will rest on the plea I have been making for poetry as nourishment and stimulus for the child's imagination.

On the other hand, while subject-matter such as clothes on a line may not appear poetically promising, some subjects are inherently 'poetical'—and should therefore be handled carefully. A line of drying clothes is a purely visual object; *Stocking and Shirt* appeals almost solely to the eye. *Bells* is a poem that makes its appeal principally to the ear.

> Hard as crystal,
>   Clear as an icicle,
> Is the tinkling sound
>   Of a bell on a bicycle.
>
> The bell in the clock
>   That stands on the shelf
> Slowly, sleepily
>   Talks to itself.
>
> The school bell is noisy
> And bangs like brass.
> 'Hurry up! Hurry up!
>   Late for class!'

But deep and distant
And peaceful to me
Are the bells I hear
Below the sea. . . .

It has often been said, and cannot be too clearly reiterated, that in poems for children an appeal should be made to *all* the senses, since one of their principal aims is the sensuous exploration of the outer world.

It should be mentioned in passing that all my poems for children have been written during the past twenty-five years during which failing eyesight has made it impossible for me to have a clear picture of either the world or the written word in visual terms. All my verse during this period has been heard by my inner ear rather than seen by my eye. All of it has had to be realized in aural form, though of course the eye of the mind, which does not suffer from myopia or glaucoma, has played its part too in shaping the formal aspects of a poem. It follows that to me sound is as important as vision, and as time goes on, increasingly more so. Aural subjects, therefore, have for me a special appeal.

Only the first part of *Bells* is quoted here, because my purpose is to exhibit the particular method employed. The aim of the poem is to draw the mind outwards towards the more inherently 'poetic' suggestion of bells by way of familiar instances. Thus first the sound of a bicycle bell, familiar to most children, is evoked—that lucent, hard tinkle; next another familiar bell-quality is hinted at—the sound of a chiming clock; thirdly, there is the harsh imperative note of the school bell. Finally the inner ear is invited to dwell on a bell sound from pure fantasy—that of the *cathédrale engloutie*, the bells of the drowned church or that of the submerged bell in Southey's *Inchcape Rock*. The everyday mind is thus gradually led outward to the larger world of fantasy and imagination.

Even larger voyages beyond the familiar can be attempted on the 'viewless wings' of poetry. Much play can be made of familiar or proverbial sayings, and poems can be written through the experimental act of taking literally a metaphorical expression. A child may be familiar with the proverbial phrase 'If pigs could fly'. If not, no matter.

> If pigs could fly, I'd fly a pig
> To foreign countries small and big—
>   To Italy and Spain,
> To Austria, where cowbells ring,
> To Germany, where people sing—
>   And then come home again.
>
> I'd see the Ganges and the Nile;
> I'd visit Madagascar's isle,
>   And Persia and Peru.
> People would say they'd never seen
> So odd, so strange an air-machine
>   As that on which I flew.
>
> Why, everyone would raise a shout
> To see his trotters and his snout
>   Come floating from the sky;
> And I would be a famous star.
> Well known in countries near and far—
>   If only pigs could fly!

Two points are worthy of note. First, the importance of the conditional mood. All possibilities stem from the word 'if'. Let us start with the condition 'If pigs could fly', and see where it leads us. Here it leads us all over the world in a kind of shorthand evocation of various foreign countries, widely dispersed. 'If' may be thought of as the simple, two-letter key to the whole realm of possibility in the youthful mind. Admittedly, 'If pigs could fly' is the hallmark of impossibility, but what is possibility but impossibility in reverse?

> If ifs and ans were pots and pans,
> There'd be no need for tinkers.

This again is no more than a comment on the part of the shrewd, prudential folk mind. But let it be turned inside out, so that children may see that there is something more entertaining than mere prudence. 'If pigs could fly, I'd fly a pig.' Just so.

> If wishes were horses beggars would ride.

Intended as a prudent discouragement to wishing, may this not also be turned inside out? Might not the challenge be accepted, and an intriguing poetic excursion into the possibility of riding on wishes be attempted?

> And I would be a famous star
> Well known in countries near and far—
> If only pigs could fly!

The second point I want to make is that the 'I' is introduced as protagonist. It is very important that adult writers should not intrude themselves into verse written for children, if they cannot do it without condescension. It is not easy to identify oneself with a child reader, and this should be done sparingly. But in every poet is a child, and if it can on occasions express its uninhibited child-wishes, so much the better. More will be said about this later. For the time being, let it be noted that the expression of a passing wish to be regarded as a 'famous star', if perhaps somewhat *risqué* on psychological grounds, may give a pleasing lift to the youthful ego. Only it must not be over-indulged.

To return to the subject of exploration.

> The furry moth explores the night,
>   The fish discover cities drowned,
> And moles and worms and ants explore
>   The many cupboards underground.
>
> The soaring lark explores the sky,
>   And gulls explore the stormy seas.
> The busy squirrel rummages
>   Among the attics of the trees.

In these eight lines the exploration is in space: night sky (the moth), day sky (the lark), under ground (moles, worms, ants), under the sea (fish), the sea's surface (gulls), treetops (the squirrel). In this wide, spatial searching the imagination is asked to range—even to dart—freely about the landscape. But exploration can also be in time. Much literature for children ranges into the future, but this kind of speculation has never appealed to me, if only because the future is uncertain. I feel more at home in certainties—in those speculations which can, if necessary, be checked by reference to written and oral sources. Smuggling is the subject of *Rum Lane*, of which this is the beginning.

> Gusty and chill
>   Blows the wind in Rum Lane,
> And the spouts are a-spill
>   With the fast-driving rain.
>
> No footfall, no sound!
>   Not a cat slithers by.
> Men of sense, I'll be bound,
>   Are at home in the dry.
>
> Tall, dark, and narrow
>   Are houses and shops—
> Scarce room for a sparrow
>   Between the roof-tops.
>
> But oh! what a history
>   Of rum and romance
> Could be made from the mystery
>   Of old Rum Lane once— . . .

Rum Lane itself is imaginary, situated perhaps in Rye or a village on the Devon Coast. Its narrowness suggests the excitement and suspense associated with the smuggling of lace and spirits to evade the vigilance of the excise officers. If this poem has a literary origin, it is probably to be found in one of the best of all smuggling stories, Russell Thorndike's brilliant *Doctor Syn*.

Historical subjects are of course inexhaustible. In *Rum Lane* it might be objected that the reader is asked to turn his mind to a conventionally 'romantic' subject. A lot of ballyhoo has been written about smuggling days, and it is necessary not to forget that a good deal of danger was involved, and that not all smugglers and highwaymen were savoury characters. Here, as an anti-romantic evocation of ancient history, is *Troy*.

> Priam is the king of ashes,
>   Heroes die and gods lament.
> Round his head his kingdom crashes.
>   Now the ten years' war is spent.
>
> Night in flames and no man sleeping,
>   Trumpets' scream across the plains,
> Charging horsemen, women weeping—
>   These are all that now remains:
>
> These and not the shouts of gladness,
>   Not the victors' face of joy,
> These I see and hear in sadness
>   When I think of fallen Troy.

The poems quoted in this chapter illustrate attempts to stretch the growing imagination and encourage it to range widely in space and time. There is perhaps not as much 'madness', as was promised by my opening words. 'Magic and mystery' have, I hope, revealed themselves. Emily Dickinson wrote:

> Much madness is divinest sense
> To a discerning eye,

but the kind of madness, the poetic unreason which appeals to children, is not easy to create. I shall have more to say later about nonsense. Meanwhile *Kingdom Cove* is an attempt to get as far away as possible from the everyday world. Poetry must do two opposed things—cause the mind to dwell on the actualities of everyday life, to see more in them than appears to the everyday mind; and at other times to get as far away from actuality as possible. *Kingdom Cove* is a poem of pure suggestion. The young reader is as likely to make sense of it, if he wants to, as the adult; or rather, he is less likely to demand that rational sense should be made of it. Stravinsky, no doubt exasperated by the failure of some critics when his music was new to make sense of it, once said, 'Only children and animals can understand my music.' *Kingdom Cove* wrote itself, so to speak, with the merest technical control by me, when my imagination had freed itself from conventional actuality.

> When I went down to Kingdom Cove,
> The cliffs were brown, the sea was mauve.
> Shadows of rocks on the clifftops lay
> As the sunset flamed across the bay.
> I saw three starfish upon the shore
> And up in the sky was one fish more.
> Birds on the tumbling waters cried
> 'Ship's away with the morning tide!'
> But the man in the lighthouse called to me,
> 'Don't go crossing the tumbling sea!'
> And I saw his telescope up to his eye
> Gazing out to the sunset sky.
> So I shouted out, 'But the night is black:
> If I don't go on, I can't go back!'
> And then a great storm cracked the sky
> And a giant sea-bird scouted by,
> He carried me off on his cloudy track
> And set me down on a dolphin's back.
> There is an island out to sea,
> Where tall trees wait to sing for me;
> Sing they will in the autumn gale,
> And there on the dolphin's back I'll sail.
> In Kingdom Cove my father stands,
> Shading his eyes with two brown hands,
> And three red starfish crumble away
> And the land-breeze blows them across the bay.

I do not know what this poem is 'about' in the conventional sense, but it would be interesting to hear the views of a psychologist. I am fairly satisfied that out of the temporary trance-like condition of mind in which it was written the poem emerges as a credible whole, with its own mood, its own area of suggestion and association. It will be noticed that the poem makes an excursion into both space and time.

CHAPTER 2

THE CHILD AS 'I'

Beech Leaves

In autumn down the beechwood path
   The leaves lie thick upon the ground.
It's there I love to kick my way
   And hear their crisp and crashing sound.

I am a giant, and my steps
   Echo and thunder to the sky.
How the small creatures of the woods
   Must quake and cower as I pass by!

This brave and merry noise I make
   In summer also when I stride
Down to the shining, pebbly sea
   And kick the frothing waves aside.

AN ADULT reader once questioned the rightness of the epithets 'crisp and crashing', as applied to the noise of a child kicking his way through beech leaves. No one who has done this in early winter, after a drought long enough to thoroughly dry the fallen leaves, would question it. The scene is part of my Buckinghamshire childhood. The third stanza connects this experience with that of kicking one's way through the shallow waves towards the deeper ones farther out.

I quote the poem here for a special purpose, that of illustrating a kind of poem often written by adults for children.[1] The pronoun 'I' is used, thus identifying the author with a child reader in recounting childhood experiences. Obviously there are pitfalls here. The rule should be that one must not invent

---

[1] As in R. L. Stevenson's *A Child's Garden of Verses.*

for the child experiences beyond his capacity. If one goes back to one's own childhood and faithfully records experiences vividly remembered, the main pitfalls are avoided. The chief dangers are those of over-sophistication on the one hand and of *fausse naiveté* on the other. Here is an example of the latter. I made it up while writing a chapter about the kind of poetry to avoid in teaching. It is a deliberate send-up of a particularly pernicious kind of verse still sometimes offered to children.

A Thought

I wish I were a bumble bee
  So merry, blithe and gay,
To buzz and hum from flower to flower
  All on a summer's day.

I wish I were a butterfly
  Upon a buttercup.
I'd flutter down the woodland paths
  And then I'd flutter up.

I wish I were—but then, oh dear!
  A sudden thought strikes me:
For if I were a butterfly,
  I could not be a bee.

I'd love to be a bumble bee
  All summer time, and so
I'm glad I'm not a butterfly
  To flutter to and fro.

This is patently specious, since no child is silly enough to wish to be a butterfly or a bee. I say nothing of the other glaring faults in this composition.

However, the experiences related in *Beech Leaves* are well within the range of any child who can walk, and the expression is simple enough for the child reader to be able to identify himself for the moment with the author.

Some might question the authenticity of the experience in
The Castle.

> One day I built a castle in the sand,
>   With battlements and pointed turret crowned.
> The tide came up, my mother called me home,
>   And so I left my castle to be drowned.
>
> That night I dreamed how in my castle tower
>   There stood a maid, distracted and forlorn,
> Who wrung her white hands, praying for the sound
>   Of horse's hooves and the deliverer's horn.

This, I think, may be defended on the ground that the child
represented as playing in the sand is a more sophisticated and
literary child, very different from the crashing extrovert of
Beech Leaves. Moreover, I was clearly writing here as an older
person remembering his childhood. The verbs are in the past
tense. The literary second stanza, recalling some folk tale, is
expressed as a dream, so that the whole experience is perfectly
credible. The language is perhaps not that of a child, but I have
no more sympathy with adult writers who write child-verse
than I have with adult artists who deliberately paint like children. There is something inherently false about this.

The Statue is a further exploration into the feelings of a child
confronted with an object of awe. One of the differences
between innocence and experience is that large inanimate objects can frighten or disconcert an imaginative child, and later
the impact weakens or fails altogether.

> On a stone chair in the market-place
> Sits a stone gentleman with a stone face.
> He is great, he is good, he is old as old—
> How many years I've not been told.
> Great things he did a great while ago,
> And what they were I do not know.
> But solemn and sad is his great square face
> As he sits high up on his square stone base.
> Day after day he sits just so,

With some words in a foreign tongue below.
Whether the wind blows warm or cold,
His stone clothes alter never a fold.
One stone hand he rests on his knee;
With the other stone hand he points at me.
Oh, why does he look at me in just that way?
I'm afraid to go, and afraid to stay:
Stone gentleman, what have you got to say?

Here an attempt is made to read the mind of the child contemplating this familiar but always disconcerting object. The child naturally has an anthropomorphic view of the statue[1] and creates for it the character of greatness and goodness. Later I found that the experience thus recalled for me remained vividly enough in my mind to be still present as the basis for an adult poem. Clearly the writing had revealed to my subconscious the symbolic character of the statue as a father- or conscience-figure, which had to be exorcized. Here is how the poem came out in the adult version. It is the only occasion on which it has happened to me to write the same poem with the two minds of innocence and experience.

The Stone Gentleman

Let us move the stone gentleman to the toadstool wood:
Too long has he disapproved in our market-place.
Within the manifold stone creases of his frock-coat
Let the woodlouse harbour and thrive.

Let the hamadryads wreathe him with bryony,
The scrolled fern-fronds greenly fantasticate,
And sappy etiolations cluster damply
About the paternal knee.

Them the abrupt, blank eyes will not offend.
The civic brow and raised, suppressive hand
Unchallenged and without affront shall manage
The republic of tall spiders.

---

[1] My three-year-old granddaughter spontaneously spoke to a small concrete lion in my garden and asked it where its mother was.

Here is part of a poem called *The Piano*. Child reader and adult author are for the time being identified. The practice of image-making when listening to music is common to both young and old. Indeed, it is a practice which makes it difficult to listen to music objectively. I once tried the experiment of asking a class of adolescents in school to listen to a suitable piece of music, Mendelssohn's *Fingal's Cave* overture, and write down, as they listened, whatever the music suggested to them. There was no compulsion. If their minds were blank (or occupied exclusively with the sounds of the music), they were not obliged to write. The results were of great interest as showing the immense variety, the lack of any unanimity, in the responses of the listeners. The multiplicity of images called up was surprising beyond my expectation.

> There is a lady who plays a piano;
> She lets me listen if I keep still.
> I love to watch her twinkling fingers
> Fly up and down in scale or trill.
>
> I love to hear the great chords crashing
> And making the huge black monster roar;
> I love to hear the little chords falling
> Like sleepy waves on a summer shore.
>
> Here comes an army with drums and trumpets,
> Now it's a battlefield, now it's a fire;
> Now it's a waterfall boiling and bubbling,
> Now it's a bird singing higher and higher . . .

That it is valid to create such images in the mind is clear from the titles of Debussy's *Préludes*—'La Cathédrale Engloutie', 'La Fille aux Cheveux de Lin' and so on. It would be interesting to play these pieces to uninstructed listeners and ask them to supply titles.

One of the purposes of poetry is to unite poet and reader in sharing a common experience. This is in some ways as important as that of giving the reader new experience. Indeed, by recreating for the reader his own perhaps forgotten life, the poet makes it new for him. Keats expresses a profound truth when he said that poetry 'should strike the reader as a wording of his own highest thoughts, and appear almost remembrance'. Not always perhaps, but often, a reader thinks 'How true' after reading a poem. The only way, ultimately, to recognize poetic truth is to test it by one's own experience. Though the form of *Boating* is a shade complicated for young readers—it was an attempt to recreate the dreamy atmosphere of the subject—the experience is a common one.

> Gently the river bore us
>   Beneath the morning sky,
> Singing, singing, singing
> Its reedy, quiet tune
>   As we went floating by;
> And all the afternoon
>   In our small boat we lay
> Rocking, rocking, rocking
>   Under the willows grey.
>
> When into bed that evening
>   I climbed, it seemed a boat
> Was softly rocking, rocking,
> Rocking me to sleep,
>   And I was still afloat.
> I heard the grey leaves weep
>   And whisper round my bed,
> The river singing, singing,
>   Singing through my head.

That should evoke a response in the minds of many children, who may also have similar experiences to recall. Nor was it, in my case, confined to childhood. After a long day of learning to drive a car, or of using the typewriter too long, I have found myself performing these actions in bed before going to sleep. It has nothing to do with dreaming, but rather with being half-awake and half-asleep.

The Grasses

The grasses nod together
   In the field where I play,
And I can never quite catch
   What they whisper and say.
Sometimes their talk
   Seems friendly and wise,
Sometimes they speak of me
   With gossip and lies.

This brief stanza contains a single thought, which might appeal
to the imagination of the introspective child—a child, some
might say with a slight sense of persecution.

Village Sounds, on the other hand, is a poem where the adult
world and the child's world meet, and the 'I' of the poem
could as easily be an adult as a child.

Lie on this green and close your eyes—
   A busy world you'll hear
Of noises high and low, and loud
   And soft, and far and near.

Amidst the squawking geese and ducks,
   And hens that cluck and croon,
The rooster on the dung-hill sings
   His shrill, triumphant tune.

A watch-dog barks to scare away
   Some sudden passer-by;
The dog wakes Mrs Goodman's Jane
   And she begins to cry.

And now the crying babe is still,
   You hear young blacksmith George
Din-dinning on his anvil bright
   Far off in his black forge.

Then on his tinkling cycle comes
   The postman with his load,
And motor-buses sound their horns
   Upon the London Road.

Sometimes a hay-cart rumbles past,
    The old sow grunts and stirs,
And in John Farrow's timber-yard
    The engine throbs and whirrs.

Just across there the schoolroom stands,
    And from the open door
You hear the sound of 'Billy Boy'
    Or else of four times four.

At half-past-three a sudden noise—
    The children come from school,
And shouting to the meadow run
    To play beside the pool.

And then, when all these sounds are still
    In the hot afternoon,
As you lie on the quiet green
    You'll hear my favourite tune.

Down from the green boughs overhead
    The gentlest murmurs float,
As hour by hour the pigeon coos
    His soft contented note.

To many this may now read like an exercise in nostalgia, but
there are still, in remote parts of Britain, blacksmiths' forges and
other manifestations of village life which, despite innovation,
are remarkably persistent. In any case, there is still some point
in the power of poetry to answer the question, 'What *were*
things like?' and not simply 'What are they like?' So *Village
Sounds* is also an exercise in imagination. The first line is an
invitation to listen:

Lie on this green and close your eyes.

The poem is in fact a conscious attempt to exclude visual
imagery and use only sound pictures. It seems to me that I

have failed noticeably in only one line, for it might be objected that there is no audible evidence that the rumbling cart is a hay-cart. But indeed the poem must not be taken too literally as a sound picture of village life, but more as a composite and selective effort by the aural imagination. If it has a concealed didactic point it is 'Use your ears. Try the experiment of supposing yourself temporarily blind.' Lastly, *Stones by the Sea* is an experiment of another kind—an experiment in personification. If stones could speak, what would they say?

> Smooth and flat, grey, brown and white,
> Winter and summer, noon and night,
> Tumbling together for a thousand ages,
> We ought to be wiser than Eastern sages.
> But no doubt we stones are foolish as most,
> So we don't say much on our stretch of coast.
> Quiet and peaceful we mainly sit,
> And when storms come up we grumble a bit.

Most, if not all, young readers can visualize stones by the sea. There is here an attempt to humanize them, to identify with them. I can imagine objections to this practice if it is carried too far. A feeling of unreality, of excessive fantasy might result. But the object of this exercise in verse is to keep the 'thoughts', 'feelings', and 'words' of the inanimate object within bounds of possibility. An anthropomorphic view of inanimate nature is, after all, ingrained in the primitive levels of consciousness. Nature is seen by the primitive mind as a witness to all human activity. In Macbeth's words:

> Stones have been known to move, and trees to speak.

This conception of nature as a witness is part of the magical view of the world, which it is an especial purpose of children's poetry to preserve and nourish.

CHAPTER 3

PEOPLE

So far I have written as if a poem were its subject-matter, and I am obliged to go on doing so until I have come to the end of what I have to say on this theme. Of course a poem is not merely—even principally—its subject-matter. Housman went so far as to say, 'Poetry is not the thing said, but a way of saying it.' This was no doubt put in an extreme form for effect. Housman wanted to insist on the importance of the non-conceptual elements in poetry. It would be juster to say, 'Poetry is the thing said *and* a way of saying it.' Content and form are inseparable, though for purposes of discussion we are bound to speak as if it were not so. I shall write of form later. In discussing many of the poems quoted so far, I might have stopped to comment on their form and technique. I preferred to ignore these elements and concentrate on what is most noticeable to a young reader.

Children are interested in content; they are not interested in form. This is a simplification. It would be more accurate to say that their interest in a poem centres in what the poem is about, and they are unaware that what the poem is about can only be conveyed by the special form of the poem—its diction, imagery, rythm and rhyme-pattern. It is necessary to underline this because, while young readers enjoy the content of a poem —or *think* they do—what appeals to me in writing for children is the formal element. A poem is nothing to me if it is no more than what it is about. A poem seems to me to be most satisfying when it is impossible to distinguish what came first into the writer's mind, so to speak, form or content. It is best when they seem, at least, to come simultaneously, when the subject-matter the writer is trying to present arrives in the mind complete with the form of expression. This must have happened in the case of *Miss Petal*.

> Sweet Miss Petal,
> She sings like a kettle,
>   Tra-la!
> Dancing, dancing
> Wherever she goes,
> She twirls about
> On the points of her toes.
>   Tra-la!
> Like a moth she dances
> On fluttery wings,
> Like a silver kettle
> She bubbles and sings,
>   Tra-la!
> Neat she is
> Like a little white rose,
> Twirling about
> On the points of her toes,
> Flitting and trilling
> Wherever she goes,
>   Tra-la!
> Dear Miss Petal,
> If only she'd settle—
>   But no!
> From morn till night,
> Day in day out,
> She turns and turns
> Like a roundabout.
> If only, if only
> She'd come to rest
> Like a bee on a bush
> A bird on a nest.
> If only, if only
> She'd sit and settle,
> Like a sensible, sober,
> Sweet Miss Petal— . . .

The lines sing themselves and dance themselves and are the embodiment of this indefatigable performer. The form—free but controlled—fits the subject and is conditioned by it. The poem was written by ear and for the ear. It is best read aloud. Here is its conclusion. The reader, or listener, undergoes a certain degree of exhaustion, as if losing breath, so the conclusion could not have been otherwise.

> . . . But no!
> Away she goes
> On her twinkling toes,
> High on her toes
> Like a tippling top,
> And nobody knows
> If sweet Miss Petal
> Who sings like a kettle
> Will ever settle
> And stop!

A good many of my poems for children are about imaginary people. They are the fictional outcome of mental excursions into the world of the grotesque. They are not so much caricatures of real people as projections, wish-objects in the manner of, say, some of the minor characters who pop up on the outskirts of Dickens' fiction.

Dr John Hearty

> Dr John Hearty,
> Though old as a fossil,
> Could dance like a fairy
> And sing like a throstle.
>
> He had not a tooth left
> To ache and decay,
> And his hair, white as snow,
> Had melted away.

He had lived in this world
A weary long while,
And all that he saw in it
Caused him to smile.

For shocking they might be,
The things that he saw,
But old Dr Hearty
Had seen worse before.

He had patients in plenty
So deathly and grim,
But their ills were all cured
With laughing at him.

For Dr John Hearty
Though old as a fossil,
Would dance like a fairy
And sing like a throstle.

Does such a character exist? No. Could he? Yes, in the mind of a child. The poem was written in the early post-war years of relief from daily fear and anxiety, and I may perhaps be forgiven for having presented a jolly family doctor who must have led, it seems, an impossibly sheltered life. I could not have written the same poem twenty years later.

That I was not, even then, lacking in awareness of the grimmer side of life is indicated by a poem written about the same time, in a very different mood.

Mrs Utter

Poor Mrs Utter,
She eats no butter.
But grisly meat and horrible pies,
With a mug of sour ale
And a loaf that is stale
And a withered brown fish with buttony eyes!

> In a black tattered skirt
> She kneels in the dirt
> And clatters her dustpan and brush on the stairs;
> But everything's dusty
> And musty and rusty,
> For the pump-handle's broken, the broom has no hairs.
>
> The roof-top is leaky,
> The window-frames squeaky,
> And out of the chimney the fledgelings fly.
> Beside the bare grate
> Lies old scraggy Kate,
> A cat with one ear and one emerald eye.
>
> Poor Mrs Utter
> Would mumble and mutter,
> 'Ah! this is no life for a Princess of Spain.
> I once had fine fare
> And silk clothes to wear,
> Ah me, shall I ever be rich again?'

Such a portrait, inviting sympathy for a displaced lady suffering from delusions of grandeur, is more in keeping with the age of rationing and austerity. *Miss Wing*, on the other hand, exists not so much in time as in a peculiarly English kind of place—the small country town bypassed by the influences of modern sales methods. Most of us know Miss Wing, who exists in a trade that seems especially resistant to the spirit of self-service. After some lines describing Miss Wing's haberdashery, the poem continues:

> . . . You push the door and the door-bell rings
> And the voice you hear is little Miss Wing's.
> 'Good-day, my dear, and how do you do?
> Now tell me, what can I do for you?
> Just half a second, please, dear Miss Gay—
> As I was saying the other day—
> Now what did I do with that so-and-so?
> I'm sure I had it a moment ago—

As I was saying—why, yes, my dear—
A very nice day for the time of year—
Have you heard how poor Mrs Such-and-such?—
Oh, I hope I haven't charged too much;
That would never do—Now, what about pink?
It's nice for children, I always think—
Some buttons to go with a lavender frock?
Why now, I believe I'm out of stock—
Well, what about these? Oh, I never knew—
I'm ever so sorry—now what about blue?
Such a very nice woman—a flower for a hat?'
And so she goes on, with 'Fancy that!'
And 'You never can tell,' and 'Oh dear, no,'
And 'There now! it only goes to show.'
And on she goes like a hank of tape,
A reel of ribbon, a roll of crêpe,
Till you think her tongue will never stop.

And that's Miss Wing of the fancy shop.

No doubt Miss Wing is on the way out, in a world where the
social side of buying is being squeezed out by streamlined
commerce. But who will be happier when she sells up to make
room for the new supermarket? While she lasts she must not
be dismissed as without utility. Why do streams of motorists
from the towns drive out on fine days to visit just such villages
and country towns where just such shops still exist?

Mr Bellairs, too, is no doubt something of a museum piece,
as he strolls in the grounds of his country mansion sniffing
exquisite blooms with his Roman nose. But once again, if he is
a fantasy, he is not wholly out of fashion, and has indeed taken
on a new life with the vogue for weekend motoring to inspect
the mansions of the impoverished great in the peace and seclu-
sion of the countryside.

In a huge hoary mansion
Lives Mr Bellairs,
With four or five stories
And hundreds of stairs.

The gates of his garden
　　Are made of wrought iron,
From the top of each gatepost
　　Glares down a great lion.

The trees in the garden
　　Are ancient and stately,
And high in their branches
　　Rooks mumble sedately.

The tails of the peacocks
　　Sweep by on the grass;
The fish in the fishpond
　　Gleam gold as they pass.

Superior tulips
　　Adorn the parterres
In the exquisite garden
　　Of Mr Bellairs.

But ah, the great mansion,
　　The dark polished floors,
The marble, the mirrors,
　　The gilt on the doors,

The bedrooms so blissful,
　　The bathrooms so roomy,
The books in the library
　　All learned and gloomy,

The cherubs on ceilings
　　And stags on the wall,
The family portraits
　　That line the great hall.

The carpets, the curtains,
　　The fat chintzy chairs—
Oh, what a palazzo
　　Has Mr Bellairs!

With such a great mansion
  And so many stairs
No wonder he's haughty
  And gives himself airs.

No wonder he's haughty
  With such an abode,
And his nose is quite straight
  Like the old Roman road.

A companion piece to *Mr Bellairs* is the portrait of *Poor Rumble*, the now almost extinct feudal head gardener, whose tyrannic skill is the obverse of the perfection of Mr Bellairs' tulip beds and velvet lawns.

Pity poor Rumble: he is growing wheezy.
  At seventy-nine years old
His breath comes hard, and nothing comes too easy.
  He finds the evenings cold.

Pity poor Rumble: winter on his noddle
  Has laid its wisps of snow;
And though about the place he scarce can toddle,
  He likes to work, I know . . .

The increasing age and stiffness of Rumble is doubtless the reason why so much of Mr. Bellairs' estate will soon be dug up and sown with grass. Meanwhile, the portrait continues with a glimpse of this remarkable craftsman in his prime.

He was the champion for fruit or tatey;
  But Rumble's famous marrow,
So huge it was and more than common weighty,
  It almost split his barrow.

Of cat and dog he was the holy terror—
  None ever plagued him twice;
And if a slug walked on his lawn in error,
  His language was not nice . . .

Many children have an aunt or a grandmother who, living on her own, is a hoarder. I do not know what the psychologists make of the hoarding instinct, but it is a fact by which children are irresistibly fascinated. *Little Minnie Mystery* is a portrait from life, seen with a child's curiosity and a child's eye for detail.

> Little Minnie Mystery has packets and parcels
>   All tied about with laces and strings,
> And all full of scraps and patches and morsels
>   And oddments and pieces and bits of things.
>
> All tied about with strings and laces
>   Are old Minnie Mystery's wonderful stores,
> And she stows them away in all sorts of places—
>   Cupboards and cases and chests of drawers.
>
> All day long you will hear her caper
>   From attic to basement, up and down stairs,
> Rummaging and rustling with tissue paper
>   And rattling keys and climbing on chairs.
>
> What does she keep in her parcels and packets?—
>   Why, buckles and beads and knobs and handles,
> Playing-cards, curtain-rings, loops, and lockets,
>   Letters and labels and Christmas-tree candles . . .

Children find no difficulty in appreciating satire, provided it is not over-subtle. Everyone knows of the kind of village where the older inhabitants are never happy about the weather, whatever it is like. Indeed, it is people everywhere, not only in the country, who enjoy exchanging symptoms. *Diddling* is this kind of simple, collective, satirical picture, not of one person but of a group.

> The people of Diddling
> Are never more than middling
> For they can't abide either cold or heat.
>   If the weather is damp,
>   It gives them cramp,
> And a touch of frost goes straight to their feet.

A thundery shower
Turns everything sour,
And a dry spell ruins the farmers' crops,
And a south-west wind
Is nobody's friend
For it blows the smoke down the chimney-tops.

Says old Mrs Morley,
'I'm middling poorly,
But thank you, I never was one to complain;
For the cold in my nose
As soon as it goes
I dursn't but say I may get it again.'

and so on.

It is sometimes fruitful to treat people in a spirit not so much of satire as of pure fantasy. I don't know whether anyone ever behaved exactly like the scandalous Mr Tom Narrow, but I see no reason why he should not exist. Stranger things are reported in the newspapers every week. At any rate, when I started to write the poem, I had no doubt of the reality of this eccentric barrow boy.

A scandalous man
Was Mr Tom Narrow,
He pushed his grandmother
Round in a barrow.
And he called out loud
As he rang his bell,
'Grannies to sell!
Old grannies to sell!'

The neighbours said,
As they passed them by,
'This poor old lady
We will not buy.
He surely must be
A mischievous man
To try for to sell
His own dear Gran.'

'Besides,' said another,
'If you ask me,
She'd be very small use
That I can see.'

I remember that while writing the poem I felt horrified at this point at the situation my mind had achieved. Possibly I was affected by the excellent relations between my own young children and their grandmother, my mother, and I had an immediate and alarming sense of having gone too far. Accordingly I put everything right by making a speedy finish:

'You're right,' said a third,
'And no mistake—
A very poor bargain
She'd surely make.'

So Mr Tom Narrow
He scratched his head,
And he sent his grandmother
Back to bed;
And he rang his bell
Through all the town
Till he sold his barrow
For half-a-crown.

There is no doubt that satire has an uncannily malign power, even in the form of light verse, and it should be used sparingly when writing for children.

Another portrait conceived in pure fantasy and in a light-hearted, carefree vein is that of the even more eccentric *Mr Kartoffel*.

Mr Kartoffel's a whimsical man;
He drinks his beer from a watering-can,
And for no good reason that I can see
He fills his pockets with china tea.
He parts his hair with a knife and fork
And takes his ducks for a Sunday walk.
Says he, 'If my wife and I should choose

> To wear our stockings outside our shoes,
> Plant tulip-bulbs in the baby's pram
> And eat tobacco instead of jam,
> And fill the bath with cauliflowers,
> That's nobody's business at all but ours.' . . .

Mrs Kartoffel is in complete accord with her husband's whimsicality, and after enumerating other curious practices in which she chooses to indulge, she concludes:

> But whatever I do that is rum or rare,
> I rather think that it's my affair.
> So fill up your pockets with stamps and string,
> And let us be ready for anything!'
> Says Mr K. to his whimsical wife,
> 'How can we face the storms of life,
> Unless we are ready for anything?
> So if you've provided the stamps and string,
> Let us pump up the saddle and harness the horse
> And fill him with carrots and custard and sauce,
> Let us leap on him lightly and give him a shove
> And it's over the sea and away, my love!'

This is of course pure nonsense, and no one is asked to take it seriously. There is, however, a note of concealed propaganda for eccentric and original behaviour of a harmless sort. The world in which children now grow up is an increasingly earnest one—a world of competitive exams and form-filling; but it will be a dull place if there is no longer any room for the occasional excursion into irresponsible and light-hearted fantasy.

In *Diddling* there was a note of country dialect, no more than a trace: and it is questionable how much dialect should have a place in children's verse. One of the maxims of the Taoists is, 'Govern a nation as you would cook a small fish'—i.e. don't overdo it. This is excellent counsel, not only in politics but in many other fields, including that of children's poetry. A little dialect is harmless and can be amusing; a lot is tedious. To any solemn reader who thinks it condescending to laugh at rural speech, I would answer, in the words of La Rochefoucauld,

'On se moque toujours de ce qu'on aime'. This is the secret of most effective humour that is not malicious—it arises from love, not from superiority. *Zachary Zed* is the portrait of a fictional character who is bound to excite one's sympathy: he is no less than the hypothetical last man on earth, and it is perfectly reasonable to depict him as a somewhat simple character.

> Zachary Zed was the last man,
>   The last man left on earth.
> For everyone else had died but him
>   And no more come to birth.
>
> In former times young Zachary
>   Had asked a maid to wed.
> 'I loves thee, dear,' he told her true,
>   'Will thou be Missis Zed?'
>
> 'No, not if you was the last man
>   On earth!' the maid replied:
> And he was; but she wouldn't give consent,
>   And in due time she died.
>
> So all alone stood Zachary,
>   ''Tis not so bad,' he said,
> 'There's no one to make me brush my hair
>   Nor send me up to bed.
>
> 'There's no one can call me wicked,
>   Nor none to argufy,
> So dang my soul if I don't per-nounce
>   LONG LIVE KING ZACHAR-Y!'
>
> So Zachary Zed was the last man
>   And the last King beside,
> And never a person lived to tell
>   If ever Zachary died.

CHAPTER 4

MAGIC

Moths and moonshine mean to me
Magic—madness—mystery.

It is a truism that the subjects for verse for children are almost unlimited. It is not always so well understood, however, that books for verse for children should illustrate this variety. Children enjoy surprise, the juxtaposition of the familiar and the strange, the reasonable and the inconsequential. Their moods change more quickly than those of adults; they live less by habit and reason than by impulse. As I said earlier, the world into which they are growing has too little time for magic, surprise, inconsequentiality. The world of the adult newspaper, though it is represented as full of incident and sensation, is increasingly predictable. Each new headline spells out no more than a nine days' wonder. Somehow the groundwork of day-to-day life in the neighbourhoods where it is lived has an obstinate tendency towards sameness. But this tendency falsifies, distorts the world of the child's imagination, the world as he would make it if his impulses had free play.

It is an educational truism that education should prepare the child for the world he is to live in. This is not so much an educational doctrine as the doctrine of hard-headed rationalists who have little time for the child's world of the imagination. If the world were in every way a satisfactory place, and one of which we adults might be proud, there would be some point in insisting that education prepared children to enter it. I would prefer to side with those who advocate education *by* freedom *for* freedom—and this includes the free play of imagination and fantasy. There will always be voices to decry the encouragement of fantasy in the minds of children and to call for the abolition of fairy tales, folklore and such 'unscientific' matter by law. But such an attitude, I think, is in itself unscientific, if to ignore the larger facts of social organization is to be unscientific. It would have been more appropriate to primitive or agrarian societies, where labour was in high and constant demand and the pressure for survival stronger, to abolish folklore and fairy tales. But such societies did not do this. Still less ought we to do so. There is now more leisure than ever, owing to technological advance, and if such leisure is not to be the source of a sterile and empty boredom, it must be a part of education to stimulate and nourish the minds and the imagination of children. There is room and time for both recreative and 'useful' studies. The two are not mutually exclusive, nor is there any evidence that the proper use of reason, the proper understanding of science and technology are inhibited by the free play of the mind in fantasy and magic. Nothing, after all, is a more characteristic fruit of a scientific age than science fiction. Whether or not the modern mind can do without science, it has shown itself unwilling to do without fiction.

All this has been said before, more eloquently and with greater thoroughness. I allude to it here by way of introducing what I have to say about magic and the supernatural in children's poetry. Of course there is what I would call natural magic everywhere—the magic of life, nature, the changing seasons, the night sky, the moods and fancies of people. Such magic it is certainly part of the function of poetry to explore. Indeed, a poem may be said to be, at best, itself a magical act or happening, constructed out of natural magic, which it illuminates, interprets, invests with verbal form and significance.

In general, then, children's poetry should be infused throughout with magic. But here I want to give some examples of magic in the more obvious, supernatural sense. To the fresh mind of a child the distinction between the natural and the supernatural is less clear-cut than to the mind of an adult. To the child, anything may happen. He should be able to accept readily a poem such as *Queer Things*, a piece of pure make-believe. Here are two stanzas from it.

> 'Very, very queer things have been happening to me
>   In some of the places where I've been.
> I went to the pillar-box this morning with a letter
>   And a hand came out and took it in . . .
>
> 'So I took my newspaper and went into the park,
>   And looked round to see no one was near,
> When a voice right out of the middle of the paper
>   Started reading the news bold and clear! . . .'

There is also the kind of magic that the Greek myths illustrate as metamorphosis. This important concept arose in the pre-scientific mind as a means of making sense and order out of the natural world. It was a means of mediating, as it were, between the gods (the supernatural) on the one hand and nature (including man) on the other. It was a way of explaining how things began. I believe that this pantheistic attitude to nature, this readiness to take an anthropomorphic view of their familiar surroundings, is common, if not universal, among children. As a boy I saw the features of giants in the profiles of trees in a familiar landscape, while their roots, if they crossed my path, were snakes, to be stepped over with care. Rationally, of course, I knew they were not; at the same time I was not consciously playing a game of make-believe. The Greeks, who invented stories, later retold by Ovid, about streams that went underground because once they had been nymphs chased by satyrs, and about Daphne, changed to a laurel to escape from Apollo —the Greeks, I am convinced, were in their time doing the same thing as the child of today. *Mumbling Hill* might be the name of a real hill, and its name might have something in common with those of the Seven Sisters or the Giants' Causeway. An attempt to explain the name might produce the verses I wrote under this title.

The two old trees on Mumbling Hill,
They whisper and chatter and never keep still.
What do they say as they lean together
In rain or sunshine or windy weather?

There were two old women lived near the hill,
And they used to gossip as women will
Of friends and neighbours, houses and shops,
Weather and trouble and clothes and crops.

And one sad winter they both took ill,
The two old women of Mumbling Hill,
They were bent and feeble and wasted away
And both of them died on the selfsame day.

Now the ghosts of the women of Mumbling Hill,
They started to call out loud and shrill,
'Where are the tales we used to tell,
And where is the talking we loved so well?'

Side by side stood the ghosts until
They both took root on Mumbling Hill;
And they turned to trees, and they slowly grew,
Summer and winter the long years through.

In winter the bare boughs creaked and cried,
In summer the green leaves whispered and sighed;
And still they talk of fine and rain,
Storm and sunshine, comfort and pain.

The two old trees of Mumbling Hill,
They whisper and chatter and never keep still.
What do they say as they lean together
In rain or sunshine or windy weather?

The nursery myth of 'Jack Frost' is a common example of
anthropomorphic personification. In the poem I wrote for the
letter 'F' in my children's alphabet, *Ragged Robin*, I raised the
homely 'Jack' to the status of a cruel king. Here it is the initial
letter 'F' which suggested the opposition between frost and

flowers. The idea of warring forces at work in nature, and a
battle of the elements, is of course primitive in origin.

Flowers are yellow
And flowers are red;
Frost is white
As an old man's head.
Daffodil, foxglove,
Rose, sweet pea—
Flowers and frost
Can never agree.
Flowers will wither
And summer's lost
When over the mountain
Comes King Frost.

White are the fields
Where King Frost reigns;
And the ferns he draws
On window-panes,
White and stiff
Are their curling fronds.
White are the hedges
And stiff the ponds.
So cruel and hard
Is winter's King,
With his icy breath
On everything.

Then up comes the sun;
Down fall the showers.
Welcome to spring
And her fellow flowers!
So sing the birds
On the budding tree,
For frost and flowers
Can never agree;
And welcome, sunshine,
That we may say
The old cruel King
Is driven away.

The Magic Seeds is a more extravagant investigation of the possibilities of the purely supernatural—too extravagant perhaps. Yet it has elements of the folklore in which some ballad fragments are so rich.

> There was an old woman who sowed a corn seed,
> And from it there sprouted a tall yellow weed.
> She planted the seeds of the tall yellow flower,
> And up sprang a blue one in less than an hour.
> The seed of the blue one she sowed in a bed,
> And up sprang a tall tree with blossoms of red.
> And high in the treetop there sang a white bird,
> And his song was the sweetest that ever was heard.
> The people they came from far and from near,
> The song of the little white bird for to hear.

There is much in the old narrative ballads that appeals to children. Especially to be enjoyed is their economy of expression and swiftness of action, their graphic concreteness of diction, their employment of repetition and use of semi-magical numbers, notably three and seven. *The Three Singing Birds* is a ballad where the action is arbitrary yet aims to appear inevitable; there is a pattern in the narrative.

> The King walked in his garden green,
>   Where grew a marvellous tree;
> And out of its leaves came singing birds
>   By one, and two, and three.
>
> The first bird had wings of white,
>   The second had wings of gold,
> The third had wings of deepest blue
>   Most beauteous to behold.
>
> The white bird flew to the northern land,
>   The gold bird flew to the west,
> The blue bird flew to the cold, cold south
>   Where never bird might nest . . .

After a year the birds return, carrying in their beaks, respectively, a pearly seed, a golden ring and a seashell. From the pearly seed, when the King plants it, rises a pearl-white maid; she kneels before him, then holds the shell to his ear, so that he hears sweet music. This is evidently a siren song inducing love for the maiden. The poem ends:

> He raised the fair maid by the hand
>   Until she stood at his side;
> Then he gave her the golden ring
>   And took her for his bride.
>
> And at their window sang the birds,
>   They sang the whole night through,
> Then off they went at break of day,
>   The white, the gold, and the blue.

Giant Thunder is another ballad, one in which anthropomorphism provides the theme, thunder and lightning being represented dramatically as the result of an exhibition of bad temper by the giant because his supper is not ready. Some children may ruefully connect this with occasions in their own experience. The poem is often used as a test piece in verse-speaking competitions, possibly because of its directness and its appeal to the ear. The essence of such a poem is economy. The theme must be presented dramatically and without being laboured or padded.

> Giant Thunder, striding home,
> Wonders if his supper's done.
>
> 'Hag wife, hag wife, bring me my bones!'
> 'They are not done,' the old hag moans.
>
> 'Not done? not done?' the giant roars
> And heaves his old wife out of doors.
>
> Cries he, 'I'll have them, cooked or not!'
> But overturns the cooking-pot.

He flings the burning coals about;
See how the lightning flashes out!

Upon the gale the old hag rides,
The cloudy moon for terror hides.

All the world with thunder quakes;
Forest shudders, mountain shakes;
From the cloud the rainstorm breaks;
Village ponds are turned to lakes;
Every living creature wakes.

Hungry Giant, lie you still!
Stamp no more from hill to hill—
Tomorrow you shall have your fill.

To a child's mind mythical characters like giants can be as real as real people, and real people can be invested with an air of the mythical. There is no rigid distinction between the imagined and the real. To a girl—and perhaps also to a boy—clothes, especially those of an earlier generation than their parents', are full of magic. *Mrs Farleigh-Fashion* is the satirical picture of a lady, human enough in her weakness, but at the same time almost legendary.

Mrs Farleigh-Fashion
Flies into a passion
If any other frock is finer than hers.
How she bobs and bounces
In her fleecy flounces,
She is like a queen in her feathers and furs.

She has a gown of flame,
Which puts ours to shame,
And one that billows like the boisterous sea.
She has another of silk,
White as morning milk,
That sighs and whispers like wind in a tree.

Mrs Farleigh-Fashion
With a long lilac sash on
Waltzed with the General at the County Ball.
When that great man of war
Fell senseless to the floor
We had to own she had conquered us all.

This is perhaps rather sophisticated for younger children, but some will respond to the picture of feminine vanity. Even quite young girls can recognize a clothes snob when they meet one. There is, however, no attempt to moralize on vanity, which is seen, not as reprehensible, but as exaggerated and therefore laughable.

There is nothing sophisticated about the quatrain on *Doctor Emmanuel*, a child's eye sketch of an impressive egghead.

Doctor Emmanuel Harrison-Hyde
Has a very big head with brains inside.
I wonder what happens inside the brains
That Doctor Emmanuel's head contains.

The comment in the last two lines, which adults may feel to contain an element of mockery, expresses the kind of thought that might be evoked in an awed younger observer. Whether or not children respond to satire depends to a large extent on the home atmosphere—the kind of reaction to the odd or comic which they learn from their parents. A sense of the grotesque or the absurd is not inborn. It comes, not from nature, but from the human context in which the child grows up. But a portrait like that of Doctor Emmanuel may appeal equally to the solemn or to the irreverent child.

CHAPTER 5

MYTH, FOLKLORE, HUMOUR, NONSENSE

WHILE there is an almost 'sick' element in some of the most popular nursery rhymes—*Three Blind Mice, Ding Dong Bell, The Queen was in the Parlour,* for instance—I would not force sick poems on children. At the same time, they can enjoy what is serious, sad and even grim. The Greek myths were not invented for children, though they come from a pre-scientific world in which there was something childlike in the popular imagination. So much of European poetry and literature is grounded in classical Greek legend that if the modern child is denied access to it, he risks missing much in the culture of his own country. In former times, when English education was firmly based on the classics, Greek ideas (often through Roman sources) were a part of every educated boy's or girl's mental world. The study of Greek has almost disappeared from the normal curriculum, and that of Latin is gradually following. The change was taking place in my youth. When at the age of fourteen I was given the alternative of studying Greek or German at school, I foolishly chose the latter, against the wise advice of my headmaster. I have always regretted it. For direct contact with the ancient world I have had to rely on Latin. All that is past praying for. The best we can do now is to give young readers a sense of the spirit of classical mythology, literature and thought through translations, adaptations and English poetry.

Many of the Greek legends tell of heroic or warlike happenings; others are concerned with accounting for the phenomena of nature—sun, moon, stars, the progress of the seasons. These legends are not always happy; about the Greek conception of happiness, for which they strove as earnestly as modern man, there is often a tinge of sadness. Young readers, if not the youngest, are ready to come to terms with sadness in literature, as a part of the realization of the totality of human experience. The story of Dis and Persephone—or Pluto and Proserpine, in Roman terms—is an example. *Pluto and Proserpine* attempts to realize, in dialogue form, something of the sadness of the Greek story in which, during the months of winter, the daughter of the corn goddess consents to live in the dark underworld, to return to earth in spring and restore warmth and fertility to the fields of men. Here are the first stanzas:

> Said Pluto the King
>   To Princess Proserpine,
> 'I will give you a marriage ring
>   If you will be my Queen.'
>
> Said she, 'What flowers spring
>   Underneath your sun?'
> Said he, 'Where I am King
>   Flowers there are none.'
>
> 'And do the gay birds sing
>   In your country?' said she,
> 'You shall hear where I am King
>   None but the owl,' said he.
>
> 'Do the people laugh and play?'
>   Asked Princess Proserpine.
> 'Are the children happy as day
>   In the meadows soft and green?'
>
> Said the King, 'There are no meadows
>   In the country where I reign.
> My people are all shadows;
>   They will not laugh again.' . . .

The aim here was to reproduce something of the stark economy of dialogue found in many of the traditional ballads. In *The Moonlit Stream* there is much more richness of imagery and perhaps more romantic suggestion. The basis of the poem is Arthurian legend, perhaps one of the richest fields for exploration by English writers. The keynote is not so much sadness as a sense of awe and wonder. It will be noticed that the 'I' of the poem could be a child—a child, that is, who had been brought up on the stories of King Arthur. Its inspiration is literary, though the images are drawn from personal observation.

A stream far off beneath the moon
    Flowed silver-bright and thin,
Winding its way like some slow tune
    Played on a violin.

The valley trees were hushed and still;
    The sky was pearly grey;
The moonlight slept upon the hill—
    As white as snow it lay.

Then softly from a ruined tower
    That rose beside the stream
A bell chimed out the midnight hour;
    And then—Oh, did I dream?—

Then all at once a long, black boat
    With neither sail nor oars
Down that bright stream began to float
    Between its shadowy shores.

No passenger nor steersman stirred
    On that enchanted thing;
But faint, unearthly-sweet, I heard
    A choir of voices sing.

It moved mysterious and serene,
    A sable-feathered swan;
It seemed the soul of some sad queen
    Was borne to Avalon.

> So in my thoughts that shadowy boat
> Will sail the moonlit river,
> And faintly I shall hear the note
> Of that sad choir for ever.

The Three Unlucky Men is a light hearted piece of nonsense inspired directly by an item of local folklore that appealed to my sense of the ridiculous when I was living at Slough in South Buckinghamshire. A local tradition, common enough, I believe, in many other districts, was that there was a treacle-mine at Chalvey. As I was then living in the parish of Upton-cum-Chalvey, I felt entitled to appropriate and adapt this piece of folklore. (Upton, long ago swallowed up in the brick-and-concrete tide of Slough, contains the beautiful church that makes a rival claim to Stoke Poges as the scene of Gray's meditations in a country churchyard.)

> Near Wookey Hole in days gone by
> Lived three unlucky men.
> The first fell down a Treacle Mine
> And never stirred again.

I don't know why the scene of this tragedy was transferred from Buckinghamshire to Wookey Hole, except that the name seemed to me inherently more comic and perhaps a more probable context for the fate of the two companions.

> The second had no better fate
> And he too is no more.
> He fell into a Custard Lake
> And could not get to shore.

> The third poor fellow, sad to say,
> He had no fairer luck,
> For he climbed up a Porridge Hill
> And half-way down got stuck.

This lugubrious recital seemed to demand some kind of conclusion, as if to make sense of three such bizarre tragedies.

Alas, alas! man is but grass,
  Let life be short or long;
And all the birds cried 'Fancy that!'
  To hear this merry song.

I have written earlier of the associations that may occur in the mind of a child between the natural scene and something read in a book. I mentioned the profiles of giants in the outlines of trees and the identification of tree roots growing across a path with snakes seen in pictures or at the zoo. *The Toadstool Wood* is made the scene of a similar legendary haunting, with associations from folk tales. This particular wood, in fact, is pictured as a possible background for what might be one of Grimm's tales. There is here an attempt to catch something of the atmosphere that always invests a well-grown wood, filled as it is with the mystery we are always ready to associate with darkness.

The toadstool wood is dark and mouldy,
  And has a ferny smell.
About the trees hangs something quiet
  And queer—like a spell.

Beneath the arching sprays of bramble
  Small creatures make their holes;
Over the moss's close green velvet
  The stilted spider strolls.

The stalks of toadstools pale and slender
  That grow from that old log,
Bars they might be to imprison
  A prince turned to a frog.

There lives no mumbling witch nor wizard
  In this uncanny place,
Yet you might think you saw at twilight
  A little, crafty face.

To some the comparison between a row of straight, etiolated toadstool stems to a prison containing a frog prince may seem far-fetched, but it is introduced to derive the maximum atmospheric effect from the subject.

A semi-legendary figure who haunts British mythology is that of Robin Hood, who has never failed to appeal to the imagination of young readers. He is probably a composite figure, part historical, part mythical—a spirit of the woods outlawed by Christianity and an actual outlaw of the Middle Ages. He is associated in the popular mind with Robin Goodfellow, or 'Mad Robin', as he is called in the title to a folk-dance tune. In the title poem to a verse alphabet I wrote under the name of *Ragged Robin*, thus making a further association with the once-common hedge flower, Robin Redbreast is identified with the spirit of Mad Robin, who once reigned in the meadows and woods of England.

> Robin was a king of men,
> A king of far renown,
> But then he fell on evil days
> And lost his royal crown.
> Ragged Robin he was called;
> He lived in ragged times,
> And so to earn his livelihood
> He took to making rhymes.
>
> A score or so of ragged rhymes
> He made—some good, some bad;
> He sang them up and down the lanes
> Till people called him mad.
> They listened for Mad Robin's songs
> Through all the countryside,
> And when they heard his voice no more
> They guessed that he had died . . .

Such a modest exercise in mythopoeia seems to me a legitimate way of introducing a collection of assorted rhymes and giving it an appropriate framework.

One of these rhymes is called *Un-*, and it exploits a series of negatives.

> Uncut is your corn, Farmer Hearn,
> Unstacked your hay,
> Unfed, your fifteen pigs
> Have run away . . .

So the poem begins, and it later appears that the reason for Farmer Hearn's neglect of his crops and herds is that he has run away to join the gipsies. ('Hearn', incidentally, was chosen because it is a common gipsy name. Perhaps, therefore, the farmer felt an irresistible compulsion to follow in the steps of his ancestors.) This poem is obviously a free variation on the theme of the popular ballad *The Raggle-Taggle Gipsies*. With this, however, *Un-* has nothing formal in common.

The moods of a writer of poems for children should vary as much and as often as those of a child. He has in mind, perhaps, his image of the child for whom he writes. In my mind the image is that of a person whose mood changes swiftly from seriousness to frivolity, from musing to smiling. If this person is to me more often a girl than a boy, it is not because I think boys less responsive to poetry; it is because girls retain longer that essentially childlike receptivity to poetry that boys lose, for some years at any rate, when they begin to be aware of their manliness. This is a pity, and it is not universally true. The teaching of poetry over the past twenty-five years has had the effect, partially, of breaking down the barrier of philistine 'toughness' that boys come up against about the age of ten or eleven. Poetry, among some boys, is still regarded as 'cissy'. If so, that is perhaps because they are given the wrong poems. The schoolboy of ten who said, some years ago, that poetry is 'all hey nonny nonny and bloody daffodils' was unconsciously criticizing, not poetry, but the wrong kind of teaching. A kind of poem that is always 'safe' with boys is that which appeals to their sense of humour. I do not mean that light verse can be regarded as an adequate substitute for poems that appeal to more serious moods and help in encouraging emotional development. But there is as much a place for fun, parody, satire in poetry as there is in life.

There was an old wife and she lived all alone
  In a cottage not far from Hitchin:
And one bright night, by the full moon light,
  Comes a ghost right into her kitchen.

About that kitchen neat and clean
  The ghost goes pottering round.
But the poor old wife is deaf as a boot
  And so hears never a sound . . .

This is the opening of a mock ballad called *The Old Wife and the Ghost*. It goes on to describe how the ghost goes berserk in the old woman's kitchen, while she sleeps through it all. Then:

Madly the ghost tears up and down
  And screams like a storm at sea;
And at last the old wife stirs in her bed—
  And it's 'Drat those mice,' says she.

Then the first cock crows and morning shows
  And the troublesome ghost's away.
But oh! what a pickle the poor wife sees
  When she gets up next day.

'Them's tidy big mice,' the old wife thinks,
  And off she goes to Hitchin,
And a tidy big cat she fetches back
  To keep the mice from her kitchen.

Another fantasy in this vein is the story of *The Two Mice*, one a Midlander, the other a Lowland Scot, who meet on the sands at Scarborough and spend the day in dancing. Their irresponsible behaviour has evil consequences.

. . . 'I'm much fatigued,' the one mouse sighed,
  'And ready for my tea.'
'Come hame awa',' the other cried,
  'And tak' a crumb wi' me.' . . .

Next day, in attempting to reach Dundee, they take a wrong turning and stray to Stoke-on-Trent.

> And there it soon began to rain,
> At which they cried full sore:
> 'If ever we get home again,
> We'll not go dancing more.'

The sequel to this doleful episode is left to the imagination.

It will have been noticed that in each of these pieces there is a touch of dialect. 'Them's tidy big mice', says the old wife, and 'Come hame awa', asks the Scottish mouse. I have already referred to the use of dialect or 'low' speech when writing of *Zachary Zed* in an earlier chapter. I would here repeat that this rather easy form of humour is permissible so long as it is not overdone. Nothing is more tedious—and, to serious people, offensive—than an excess of Loamshire dialect or music-hall Scots. This is because it is, basically, a form of facetiousness, or self-conscious playing to the gallery, than which few literary devices are more tiresome. It is a sobering thought that there are fewer good humorists than good poets and serious novelists.

Another pitfall for writers of verse for children is the temptation to be cosy about animals. Readers may judge for themselves whether I have altogether avoided this in *Rabbit and Lark*.

> 'Under the ground
>   It's rumbly and dark
> And interesting,'
>   Said Rabbit to Lark.

> Said Lark to Rabbit,
>   'Up in the sky
> There's plenty of room
>   And it's airy and high.'

> 'Under the ground
>   It's warm and dry.
> Won't you live with me?'
>   Was Rabbit's reply.

'The air's so sunny.
    I wish you'd agree,'
Said the little Lark,
    'To live with me.'

But under the ground
    And up in the sky,
Larks can't burrow
    Nor rabbits fly . . .

So Skylark over
    And Rabbit under
They had to settle
    To live asunder.

And often these two friends
    Meet with a will
For a chat together
    On top of the hill.

This is perhaps a trifle self-indulgent, giving in to the widespread
delight on the part of children (something we outgrow at an
early age) in imaginary conversations between animals. Indeed,
the treatment of animals in children's verse is a severe test of
the writer's power of restraint and of sympathy with animal
nature. The temptation to anthropomorphize has to be held in
check. I may say in passing that, in the field of prose, I have
always found Beatrix Potter a much 'purer' writer in this res-
pect than either Kenneth Grahame or A. A. Milne. I should be
hard put to it to say why. My defence of *Rabbit and Lark* would
be that it is a sincere attempt to explore in simple dramatic
terms the essential difference in the way of life of two creatures
of nature. However desirable the need for companionship, one
is limited by one's element—though a compromise is sometimes
feasible.

Mick is possibly more successful. Children, it need hardly be
said, attach strong sentiments to domestic pets, and the aim in
this piece has been to convey sentiment without sentimentality.

C

Mick my mongrel-O
Lives in a bungalow,
Painted green with a round doorway.
With an eye for cats
And a nose for rats
He lies on his threshold half the day.
He buries his bones
By the rockery stones,
And never, oh never, forgets the place.
Ragged and thin
From his tail to his chin,
He looks at you with a sideways face.
Dusty and brownish,
Wicked and clownish,
He'll win no prize at the County Show.
But throw him a stick,
And up jumps Mick,
And right through the flower-beds see him go!

I am not a writer who has always been content to take the physical world as I find it and keep my eye strictly on the natural object. There is an irresistible temptation to invent— to add to the natural history of the world animals that the creator forgot to make. Here one can have free play with physiology and instinctual behaviour, taking care not to stray too far from the area of what is possible. In writing *Prefabulous Animiles*, a book of outlandish beasts, I kept at the back of my mind Aristotle's dictum that the impossible probable is to be preferred to the possible improbable. In other words, the wilder the unreality, the greater the credibility. Nature, it may be argued, can afford to create the possible improbable; a mere poet cannot. For instance, the improbability of the giraffe, the kangaroo or the dromedary has always seemed to me inartistic. Imagine a world in which the giraffe had not been created: if a writer described such an animal minutely, with an accompanying sketch, you would not be impressed. But the Hippocrump, I claim, is, in its horrific way, much more credible.

Along the valley of the Ump
Gallops the fearful Hippocrump.
His hide is leathery and thick;
His eyelids open with a *click*!
His mouth he closes with a *clack*!
He has three humps upon his back;
On each of these there grows a score
Of horny spikes, and sometimes more.
His hair is curly, thick and brown;
Beneath his chin a beard hangs down.
He has eight feet with hideous claws;
His neck is long—and O his jaws!
The boldest falters in his track
To hear those hundred teeth go *clack*!
The Hippocrump is fierce indeed,
But if he eats the baneful weed
That grows beside the Purple Lake,
His hundred teeth begin to ache.
Then how the creature stamps and roars
Along the Ump's resounding shores! . . .

Of course no archaeological anatomist would accept this, but I don't write for anatomists. A more sympathetic creation perhaps is offered in the intimate and somewhat pathetic figure of the Doze. (A publisher friend of mine was convinced that this unfortunate creature was a portrait of himself. I could only reassure him by telling him that the identification was in his mind, not in mine.)

Through Dangly Woods the aimlesss Doze
A-dripping and a-dribbling goes.
His company no beast enjoys.
He makes a sort of hopeless noise
Between a snuffle and a snort.
His hair is neither long nor short;
His tail gets caught on briars and bushes,
As through the undergrowth he pushes.
His ears are big, but not much use.
He lives on blackberries and juice

And anything that he can get.
His feet are clumsy, wide and wet,
Slip-slopping through the bog and heather
All in the wild and weepy weather.
His young are many, and maltreat him;
But only hungry creatures eat him.
He pokes about in mossy holes,
Disturbing sleepless mice and moles,
And what he wants he never knows—
The damp, despised and aimless Doze.

Such imaginary portraits aim, of course, to arouse some simple
emotion on the reader's part. Here it is a kind of contemptuous
sympathy. In other 'Animiles' it is a nameless fear or horror.
The Snitterjipe is not to be taken too seriously.

In mellowy orchards, rich and ripe,
Is found the luminous Snitterjipe.
Bad boys who climb the bulging trees
Feel his sharp breath about their knees;
His trembling whiskers tickle so,
They squeak and squeal till they let go.
They hear his far-from-friendly bark;
They see his eyeballs in the dark
Shining and shifting in their sockets
As round and big as pears in pockets.
They feel his hot and wrinkly hide;
They see his nostrils flaming wide,
His tapering teeth, his jutting jaws,
His tongue, his tail, his twenty claws.
His hairy shadow in the moon,
It makes them sweat, it makes them swoon;
And as they climb the orchard wall;
They let their pilfered pippins fall . . .

By doing so, they divert the attention of the monster from
themselves to their booty, and in munching apples the creature
forgets about the boys, who are able to sneak home. In order
to create an impression of vague horror, a writer should aim at

the greatest possible precision of language and the most careful selection of graphic and telling details.

The Blether is a long narrative poem in ballad form. It is, in fact, a parody of the border ballads, probably written after a surfeit of reading Child. It is a piece of nonsense based on the emotion of indefinable fear. The aim was to secure the maximum of suspense and apparent authenticity of experience, while keeping the exact nature and appearance of the 'animile' in question wholly undefined. In this instance, I specially asked the artist, Edward Ardizzone, not to depict the creature in his drawings.

In true ballad style the poem opens with a direct command. The speaker and the circumstances are revealed only in the third stanza.

> 'Up, up, my sons, my daughter dear—
>   Go forth this day together!
> To horse, to horse! Take hound and horn
>   And hunt the baneful Blether.
>
> 'Last night I felt his baneful breath
>   Upon my forehead chill.
> These spots so red upon my head
>   I fear may work me ill.'
>
> Thus groaning on his bed of pain,
>   We heard the old man sigh:
> 'Unless you kill the fexious beast,
>   Tomorrow I shall die!' . . .

The chase begins, brothers and sister being mounted on assorted steeds.

> We hunted high, we hunted low,
>   We sought through heath and heather.
> Through sun and shade the fox-hounds bayed—
>   They smelt the noxious Blether . . .

As the chase goes on, the participants gradually drop out,

either from weariness or because their horses fall lame. Next the swiftest of the hounds are lost in a foaming river.

> Right soon we came to Woeful Woods,
>   And there the Beast we spied.
> 'Press on, press on!' cried Brother John.
>   'I can no further ride.'

With all the arbitrariness of a true ballad of action, another brother is out of the hunt. Meanwhile, the others continue hot on the trail of the noisome beast. A storm breaks out:

> The thunderbolts came crashing down,
>   The thunder groaned full sore.
> 'Now strike me dead!' cried Brother Ned,
>   'For I can ride no more.' . . .

After further disasters, only the narrator and his sister are left in the chase, which ends right beside the ancestral home, with the Blether dead in the grounds, presumably from exhaustion. The bane is exorcized, and this happy conclusion is celebrated with a joyful feast. I have the feeling that this sort of thing is more fun to write than to read; but at least, as a parodic border ballad, it has the merit of showing the weaknessess as well as some of the strengths of that form.

I will end this section with a few words about writing narrative verse. I have never found this easy, partly because it seems to me that there is less room for experiment than with non-narrative poetry. Narrative poetry held the field for many years before the development of prose, and most of its functions have long ago been taken over by prose. I wonder, for instance, how much of *The Canterbury Tales* would have been written in verse if the tradition of narrative prose had existed in England in Chaucer's century. Nevertheless, children like stories in verse, and I have more than once attempted them. The forms of narrative verse seem to me restrictive, and most of my verse stories turn out like ballads, mock-ballads or folk songs. In *Roundabout* I have tried to get away from this.

> At Midsummer Fair on a galloping pony
> We saw the last of little Tony.
> He spurred her sides and said, 'Hurroo!'
> And over the heads of the crowd he flew . . .

The story is a variation on the theme of the flying carpet, which transports the traveller high over the varied countries of the earth.

> He saw the ships and the coast of France
> And sailor boys in a hornpipe dance . . .

Tony crosses Europe and the Mediterranean and reaches the African sky. Here he sees

> . . . lone grey mountains and deserts brown
> And giant cataracts tumbling down,
> Giraffes and lions and chimpanzees
> And monkeys swinging among the trees . . .

Finally the horse changes course and lands on an island off the coast of East Africa. Here Tony decides to stay for a year

> Where never a white boy stayed before . . .

Tony is left with the general intention of flying home some day.

As a story this is not wholly satisfactory. It lacks incident and, in fact, turns out to be no more than a highly coloured travelogue, an occasion for varied descriptive writing. Except in brief poems I have not solved to my satisfaction the problem of writing narrative poems that do not read like ones written before by someone else. The longest and most sustained I have attempted is one for very young readers and listeners called *Jackie Thimble*. This is much more ambitious than *Roundabout* in action and form, but the effort it cost has so far discouraged me from trying again to achieve a long narrative poem.

CHAPTER 6

WORD PLAY, RIDDLES, SONGS

Uriconium

There was a man of Uriconium
Who played a primitive harmonium,
Inventing, to relieve his tedium,
Melodies high, low, and medium,
And standing on his Roman cranium
Amidst a bed of wild geranium,
Better known as pelargonium,
Since with odium his harmonium
Was received in Uriconium.

Part of the pleasure of writing poems for young readers is that it can be a game—a game with words. From my earliest years I have, like many others, played word-games with myself. This can be more constructive and satisfying than solving or making up crossword puzzles. It can give pleasure to young readers. *Uriconium* is a piece of near-nonsense based on the discovery of a number of words in English taken direct from Latin and ending in -ium. For all their ordinariness they manage somehow to remain not quite English. They make a contrast with the more English-sounding words in the poem. It is not difficult to compose such a piece. It is only necessary to assemble all the -ium words you can think of—harmonium, tedium, medium, and so on—arrange them in a series of rhymed pairs and make the most plausible sense out of them. The rhyme scheme, it will be noticed, becomes irregular towards the end, and there are a number of -ium words that are not used, such as 'encomium' and 'podium'. *Uriconium*, the Roman camp near the modern city of Shrewsbury, seemed a fitting setting for this little extravaganza.

The composing of a set of twenty-seven rhymes (one for each letter and a title-piece) in the form of an alphabetical series provided an excellent opportunity for verbal athletics. These were written with one eye on the artist who was to do the illustrations. *Yonder*, for instance, is a sad little rhyme, very apt for illustration. I quote it here because it is an example of a game with a single word. It was suggested to my mind by a small, witty picture I saw long ago in a French newspaper. The sketch was of a little man fishing at the edge of a stream, with two fish with their heads out of the water. One is saying to the other: 'Il me semble que ce pauvre bonhomme a beaucoup vieilli depuis l'année dernière.'

> Through yonder park there runs a stream;
> By yonder stream there sits a man;
> As yonder man in silence sits
> He catches fish as best he can.
>
> While yonder fish, one, two and three,
> Through yonder limpid waters steer,
> Why does yon silent fisherman
> Drop first a sigh and then a tear?
>
> Why does he cast yon fishing line
> Again, again, and all for naught?
> It is because yon little fish,
> For all his care, will *not* be caught.

A rather simpler game is offered by *The Song of D*.

> Who will sing me the song of D?
> How many dancers can you see?
> Dinah, Deborah, Duncan, Dick,
> And Dan with his fiddle and fiddling-stick.
>   Sing it low, sing it high,
> Till the glory shines in the western sky . . .

Next, a list of cities: Dublin, Dartmouth, Darlington, Deal and Dover. Next, flowers: daffodil, dahlia, daisy, and so on. Animals beginning with D are: dodo, dromedary, dingo, duck, dragon.

There is no necessary end to such a series, and no obvious connection except the ubiquity of the initial D.

The letter J is treated in similar fashion, except that here there is an attempt at some sort of progression.

> Jerusalem, Joppa, Jericho—
> These are the cities of long ago . . .

This is followed by a series of jewels—jasper, jacinth, jet and jade; by flowers and bushes; by a sequence of boys' and girls' names; by the three J months; by clothes—jacket, jerkin, jeans; by the names of animals; by a list of dishes for a sweet-tooth— jellies, jumbles, junkets, jam; by a series of verbs:

> To jig, to jaunt, to jostle, to jest—
> These are the things that Jack loves best . . .

By this time it appears what the real significance of the letter J is, and the rhyme concludes:

> Jazz, jamboree, jubilee, joke—
> The jolliest words you ever spoke.
>
> From A to Z and Z to A
> The joyfullest letter of all is J.

Kay is something more than a mere tongue-twister. It evokes, through a rhyme on the Seneschal Sir Kay, the atmosphere of Arthurian romance.

> Kay, Kay,
> Good Sir Kay,
> Lock the gate
> Till dawn of day,
> So to keep bad men away.
>
> This is the Keep,
> And this is the key.
> Who keeps the key
> Of the Keep?
>   Sir Kay.

Kay, Kay,
Good Sir Kay,
Lock the gate
Till dawn of day.

The bell has rung
To evensong.
The priest has blessed
The kneeling throng.
In bower and hall
To bed have gone
Knights and squires,
All and one,
Lords and ladies
One and all,
Groom in kitchen,
Steed in stall.

Kay, Kay,
Good Sir Kay,
Lock the gate
Till dawn of day.
On shield and scabbard
Starlight falls,
Stalk the watchmen
Along the walls.
From hazel thicket
The screech-owl calls.
By dying fire
The boarhounds sleep.
Sir Kay, Sir Kay,
Lock fast the Keep.
This is the Keep,
And this is the key.
Who keeps the key
Of the Keep?
                    Sir Kay.

Kay, Kay,
Good Sir Kay,
Lock the gate
Till dawn of day,
So to keep bad men away.

It is late, late.
Lock fast the gate.

I have always been delighted by the game of asking riddles—
a game as old as any we know of. Every child is pleased with
the rhyme riddles he finds in his first book of verse:

A house full, a hole full—
You cannot catch a bowl full.

It does not spoil his pleasure when he has to be told that the
answer is 'Smoke'. More imaginative and poetic is the 'Egg'
riddle:

In marble halls as white as milk,
Lined with a skin as soft as silk,
Within a fountain crystal-clear
A golden apple doth appear.
No doors there are to this stronghold,
Yet thieves break in and steal the gold.

Many of the Anglo-Saxon riddles, which must be of much
greater antiquity, are not only ingenious and elaborate, but
also strikingly poetic. Their solution by an audience, as well as
their composition, call for a skill beyond that of children. Here
is the *Riddle of Sun and Moon*, as translated by Gavin Bone:

I saw a creature sally with booty,
Between its horns bearing treasures amazing.
'Twas a bright cup of the air,
A brave pipkin-thing
Adorned with delicate, darting rays.
This plunder gay for a bower it would take
Spoil of the air to its palace dim,
And, cunning, would build a room of its own in heaven.

Over the wall an arrogant being
Sprang up, though common to all men's sight is he.
He snatched the booty, drove the other home,
Wisp of a pilgrim; and westwards itself
The cruel creature went careering on.
Dust blew up. Dew came down.
The night followed after. But never a man
Knew where the wandering thing had gone.

And here is the hauntingly beautiful anonymous riddle of *Snow and Sun*:

> White bird, featherless,
> Flew from Paradise,
> Pitched on the castle wall;
> Along came Lord Landless,
> Took it up handless,
> And rode away horseless to the King's white hall.

Based on the two contrasting qualities of the wind, violence and gentleness, here is a series of four couplets:

The Wind

> I can get through a doorway without any key,
> And strip the leaves from the great oak tree.
>
> I can drive storm-clouds and shake tall towers,
> Or steal through a garden and not wake the flowers.
>
> Seas I can move and ships I can sink;
> I can carry a house-top or the scent of a pink.
>
> When I am angry I can rave and riot;
> And when I am spent, I lie quiet as quiet.

Fire is more akin to the Anglo-Saxon riddle, and like all such rhymes, it aims at stimulating the child's imagination. Riddles of this kind are something he will enjoy trying to compose for himself, and perhaps for his friends.

Hard and black is my home,
Hard as a rock and black as night.
Scarlet and gold am I,
Delicate, warm and bright.

For long years I lie,
A prisoner in the dark,
Till at last I break my fetters
In a rush of flame and spark.

First a tree and then a rock
The house where I sleep.
Now like a demon
I crackle and hiss and leap.

The multiple riddle, involving the identification of more than one disguised person or object, is a not very common, but widely enjoyed, form. Here is the ingenious traditional rhyme about a milkmaid at work:

Two legs sat upon three legs,
With four legs standing by;
Four were then drawn by ten:
Read my riddle ye can't,
However much ye try.

As most children enjoy this sort of intelligence test, I composed *The Intruder*, in which a number of creatures are mentioned by certain of their characteristics. It is for the reader to identify them.

The Intruder

Two-boots in the forest walks,
Pushing through the bracken stalks.

Vanishing like a puff of smoke,
Nimbletail flies up the oak.

Longears helter-skelter shoots
Into his house among the roots.

At work upon the highest bark,
Tapperbill knocks off to hark.

Painted-wings through sun and shade
Flounces off along the glade.

Not a creature lingers by,
When clumping Two-boots comes to pry.

Spells is a rhyme, or rather a series of couplets, similar to
The Wind, quoted above, but dealing, not with varying aspects
of one phenomenon, but with a number of different objects.
The trouble with this kind of multiple series is that it tends to
lack any real unifying feature. The first couplet of *Spells* is:

I dance and dance without any feet—
This is the spell of the ripening wheat . . .

It is not difficult to go on in this vein—indeed, it is difficult to
stop. The next two couplets deal with grass and apples, a
reasonable progression from wheat. Next come three couplets
about 'the brook', 'the river' and 'the waterfall':

. . . I fall for ever and not at all—
This is the spell of the waterfall.

Without a voice I roar aloud—
This is the spell of the thundercloud . . .

Perhaps it would have been better to stop there, but the mood
was on, and I added further spells for 'goat', 'cuckoo', 'flames'
and 'book'. I would not like to claim a high degree of unity
for this series, but an ingenious apologist could argue for a
certain progression of images.

Indeed, it is possible, even in a catalogue poem, to make some
sort of progression in the imagery. *Yonder*, it will be recalled,
is a poem exploiting the possibilities of a single word: the
title-word has something of an incantatory function. I have
several times used single words as pegs on which to hang a
series of images—or rather, as hooks to fish up images or ideas

having at least one quality in common. Here are the first two couplets of *Slowly*:

> Slowly the tide creeps up the sand,
> Slowly the shadows cross the land.
> Slowly the cart-horse pulls his mile,
> Slowly the old man mounts the stile . . .

The images of the rising tide, the moving shadows, the homing cart-horse and the old man call up a feeling of evening. The remaining two couplets run:

> . . . Slowly the hands move round the clock,
> Slowly the dew dries on the dock.
> Slow is the snail—but slowest of all
> The green moss spreads on the old brick wall.

Here there is something of a morning feeling, with the snail at large and the dew drying on the broad leaves of the dock. All the movements so far, however slow, are perceptible, and the poem is now rounded off with an image of imperceptible movement—that of the moss spreading year by year on an old wall.

Shiny, on the other hand, is more discursive. At line 4 there is a change of imagery from that of nature in early summer to something abruptly different.

> Shiny are the chestnut leaves
>   Before they unfold.
> The inside of a buttercup
>   Is like polished gold.
> A pool in the sunshine
>   Is bright too,
> And a fine silver shilling
>   When it is new.
> But the round, full moon,
>   So clear and white,
> How brightly she shines
>   On a winter night!

> Slowly she rises,
>   Higher and higher,
> With a cold clear light
>   Like ice on fire.

It might be objected that the shifts in imagery are too abrupt.
But can it be denied that this is how the mind works, at any
rate in idleness or in childhood? Such mental leaps are the
basis of metaphor.

It is not certain whether a poem such as *Shiny*, with its
reference to a new shilling—that is, an old one—and the moon
as feminine, can have any appeal to an up-to-date young reader
of today. If so, then what is to be said for a rhyme such as *A
Farthing and a Penny?*

> For a farthing and a penny you cannot buy much
> You cannot buy a parrot nor rabbits in a hutch.
> You can buy sugary sweets but not very many,
> Oh what shall I buy with my farthing and a penny?

But one need not be too serious about a mere jingle, written in
the spirit of the nursery rhymes, where archaisms are accepted
as part of their magic.

> You owe me five farthings,
> Say the bells of Saint Martin's.

Does any child ask, even now, and even if he does not know,
what 'five farthings' are?

Songs and jingles like this are the essence of verse for the
very young. It would be a solemn world in which mermaids
were banished as impossible fictions.

> She sits by the sea in the clear, shining air,
>   And the sailors call her Moonlight, Moonlight;
> They see her smoothing her wavy hair
>   And they hear her singing, singing.
>   The sea-shells learn their tunes from her
> And the big fish listen with never a stir
>   To catch the voice of Moonlight, Moonlight,
> And I would hark for a year and a year
>   To hear her singing, singing.

Any child with a musical inner ear can respond to a simple song like this, which is intended, as it were, to sing itself. Technically this is an experiment in non-rhyme, where the end of the fourth line disappoints the expectation set up by the end of the second. The device of word-repetition ('Moonlight, Moonlight' and 'singing, singing') is used as a substitute for rhyme. This song has not, to my knowledge, been set to music, but *Run a little* is a rhyme that has attracted more than one composer for children.

> Run a little this way,
>   Run a little that!
> Fine new feathers
>   For a fine new hat
> A fine new hat
>   For a lady fair—
> Run around and turn about
>   And jump in the air . . .
>
> Run a little this way,
>   Run a little that!
> White silk ribbon
>   For a black silk cat.
> A black silk cat
>   For the Lord Mayor's wife—
> Run around and turn about
>   And fly for your life!

This clearly resembles the kind of singing-game rhymes that were collected in the last century by Lady Gomme and are still being collected in some districts of Britain. The essence of them is a combination of apparent arbitrariness and a kind of inner logic, a progression of images leading up naturally to an injunction to act. *Run a little* is perhaps more of a dance-rhyme than a singing-game.

The Musical Box is a *jeu d'esprit* based on a very simple feature. It is (like the folk-song about *The Tree in the Wood*) circular in form, ending where it begins.

Mary, Mary come and listen a minute!
Here's a little wooden box with music in it.
There are little bells inside, and they tinkle and play,
And 'Early One Morning' are the words they say.

Early one morning to the woods we will run,
And see the sweet flowers at the rising of the sun.
We will join hands together and dance in a ring
And 'The Bluebells of Scotland' is the tune we will sing . . .

The bluebells of Scotland ring the tune of 'The Miller of Dee';
the miller whistles 'The Merry Widow'; the widow sings 'The
Vicar of Bray'; the vicar sings 'Annie Laurie'; Annie sings a
song called 'Mary, Mary', and by this means the opening
couplet is reached once more. This of course is highly contrived, and it would have taken little ingenuity to extend it
indefinitely. This could have been tedious, and it is important
that such contrivance should be used economically. *The
Musical Box* consists of only twenty lines. All children love a
musical box, and it seemed right to compose a song about one.

I have not said a lot about the subject of emotion in children's
verse, though it should have been apparent that I have attempted at least to awaken and satisfy the generalized emotions of
wonder, curiosity and a sense of magic. An emotion I have
found myself exploiting a number of times is that of awe and
even fear; a *frisson* of mild or playful horror is enjoyed by most,
if not all, children. This should never be over-exploited. Young
readers need not (whatever the purveyors of horror for children think) be subjected to nightmares. The opening poem
of *Prefabulous Animiles*—the title piece—begins:

> Let no one suppose
> That the creatures he knows—
> The robin, the rat . . .

The list of everyday creatures continues for some lines until:

> Let no one suppose that creatures like those
> Are ALL that the Animal Kingdom can show:
> NO!

> When the woods rumble low
> And the storm-clouds ride by in the purplish sky,
> At the corners of dreams,
> Round the edges of sleep,
> There's something that *seems* to be going to creep,
> To crawl or to climb, to lumber or leap
> Round the corners of dreams and the edges of sleep.
> You cannot be sure that you fastened the door,
> You cannot be certain that under the curtain
> There isn't a tail or a paw or a claw . . .

I do not think that this, though calculated to make a sensitive skin creep, is going too far. Imaginative children already know it is true and invent such things for themselves. They cannot help it. Neither this poem nor the book it introduces has to my knowledge been called morbid. Its very exaggerations, its extravagance of language, take the edge off the *frisson*, and the rhyme and rhythm lull the awakened senses and put the book at a distance from the everyday world.

As for more adult emotions—those of love or of sorrow, for instance—I have always thought it better not to dwell on these: let children come to them in their own time, through poetry written for older people. Yet there is always the child who is thoughtful beyond his age, and for him such a poem as *Trees in the Moonlight* may give some relief or find an echo in some half-articulated feeling in himself.

> Trees in the moonlight stand
> Still as a steeple,
> And so quiet they seem like ghosts
> Of country people—
>
> Dead farmers and their wives
> Of long, long ago,
> Haunting the countryside
> They used to know;
>
> Old gossips and talkers
> With tongues gone still;

> Ploughmen rooted in the land
>   They used to till;
>
> Old carters and harvesters,
>   Their wheels long rotten;
> Old maids whose very names
>   Time has forgotten . . .

This invites an introspective reader to think beyond his own immediate experience and to share the feelings of others beyond the island of his immediate self. The poem concludes:

> Ghosts are they hereabouts;
>   Them the moon sees,
> Dark and still in the fields
>   Like sleeping trees.
>
> Long nights in autumn
>   Hear them strain and cry,
> Torn with a wordless sorrow
>   As the gale sweeps by.
>
> Spring makes fresh buds appear
>   On the old boughs,
> As if it could to their old wishes
>   These ghosts arouse.
>
> Trees in the summer night
>   By moonlight linger on
> So quiet they seem like ghosts
>   Of people gone,
>
> And it would be small wonder
>   If at break of day
> They heard the far-off cock-crow
>   And fled away

Finally I would mention two poems made up for an especial purpose—that of choral verse-speaking. At one time I was in charge of some students at a College of Education, and they expressed dissatisfaction with some of the material offered by their textbooks for this purpose. To be suitable for choral speech a poem must contain dramatic elements—a form that allows of being broken up into separate lines or stanzas to be spoken by different voices, either singly or in groups. I should say, not so much 'allows of' (since this invites distortion by a too-ingenious teacher), as 'demands'.

The first five lines of *Cows* are spoken by a group:

> Half the time they munched the grass, and all the time they lay
> Down in the water-meadows, the lazy month of May,
>> A-chewing,
>> A-mooing,
> To pass the hours away. . . .

There follow three four-line stanzas recording the laconic and sleepy dialogue of two contented cows:

> 'Nice weather,' said the brown cow.
>   'Ah,' said the white.
> 'Grass is very tasty.'
>   'Grass is all right.' . . .

Each stanza of dialogue is followed by the refrain of the opening five lines. The aim of the solo speakers is, of course, to sound as cowlike as possible without sacrificing distinctness of articulation.

The other poem I wrote expressly for choral speaking is *The Ceremonial Band*. Both this and *Cows* have been set to music.

> The old King of Dorchester,
> He had a little orchestra,
> And never did you hear such a ceremonial band. . . .

This is the refrain, which is chorused after each stanza. It was no doubt suggested by the fact that the children for whose use it was intended were girls at Dorchester High School. After the refrain the song is built up cumulatively, as follows:

'Tootle-too,' said the flute,
'Deed-a-reedle,' said the fiddle,
For the fiddles and the flutes were the finest in the land. . . .

Each of the lines referring to a different orchestral instrument is spoken by a solo voice, or a small group, the whole company coming in with the refrain. Obviously the poem also invites the addition of action or mime. After each refrain a new musical instrument is added, until the whole orchestra is brought in, and the song concludes:

The old King of Dorchester,
He had a little orchestra,
And never did you hear such a ceremonial band.
'Pah-pa-rah,' said the trumpet,
'Zoomba-zoom,' said the bass,
'Pickle-pee,' said the fife,
'Pump-a-rum,' said the drum,
'Tootle-too,' said the flute,
'Deed-a-reedle,' said the fiddle,
For the fiddles and the flutes were the finest in the land!
Oh! the fiddles and the flutes were the finest in the land!

PART II

Technique in Children's Poetry

CHAPTER 7

RHYTHM, METRE, VERSE FORMS

In writing of poetry it is necessary to discuss subject-matter and technique as if they were two separate things. It is unavoidable, but it has one disadvantage: it creates in the minds of some readers the idea that a poem is a piece of prose written in verse. It cannot be too strongly stated that a good poem, however much it may have been shaped or altered in the process of composition, emerges *as a poem*, not as a thought, a story, a description to which a verse form is applied, as it were, from the outside. I once offered a story for illustration to a publisher whose reader was in many ways intelligent and discriminating. She asked me to 'rewrite it in verse'. I had to point out that if I had wanted to write a verse story, I would have done so and would have conceived of it quite differently from the start. It was subsequently published successfully in the form in which I had first written it. My point is, however, not that a poem writes itself, but that it presents itself, perhaps only vaguely at first, to the mind of the writer, not as thought, description or story, but as words—rhythm, image, diction. Its starting point may indeed be a word, an image, a line or even only a rhythm.

So much for what I may call the 'automatic' element in writing. When the poem has formed in the writer's mind in embryo, in outline, in general direction, the act of composition has begun, but it is completed in the act or process of writing. It is then that choice has to be made—choice of rhythm, if that has not already been made; choice of a verse form; choice of words and images within the framework of the chosen scheme. It is a truism that no verse writer would conceive of a sad poem in a jolly rhythm or a light and airy song in a ponderous rhythm. Yet I have always felt that Byron showed a lack of judgement, or perhaps of aural sensitivity, in writing of the destruction of the armies of the Assyrian Sennacherib in a metrical form suggestive of frivolity. His anapaestic measure was all right for the horse-ride, but unsuitable for the sudden death by plague of a vast army.

Between a near-mechanical regularity and an excessive freedom in metre and rhythm a writer has infinite choice. He has also a wide choice between the simplest possible verse form—the octosyllabic couplet, for instance, and the ballad stanza—and sophisticated stanza forms such as those used by Herrick or Hardy. These matters are determined by instinct. They concern the poet, but not the reader, except as they affect his immediate response to the poem. If he is unusually thoughtful and analytical, he will be conscious of the author's technical achievement or failure, even as he reads. But it is not part of the author's purpose to obtrude his technique. Indeed, the better the poem, the more immediate will be the appeal of its subject-matter to a young reader: the reader does not need to be aware, as the writer is, that content and form are one and inseparable.

> There met two mice at Scarborough
>   Beside the rushing sea,
> The one from Market Harborough,
>   The other from Dundee.
>
> They shook their feet, they clapped their hands,
>   And twirled their tails about;
> They danced all day upon the sands
>   Until the stars peeped out. . . .

This is the beginning of *The Two Mice*, already referred to, a narrative poem in simple ballad metre. This form is especially suitable for children's verse, because it is direct and easy to read aloud. It is traditional, and young readers will already have met it in many familiar examples. One reason why it has stood the test of centuries is that it is easily memorized and has

that inevitability of cadence and rhyme-scheme which is a
recommendation to an unsophisticated ear.

I have mentioned the care with which frightening subjects
should be introduced—more in the spirit of a game than with
any wish to inspire horror. The very familiarity—almost the
homeliness—of the ballad metre takes the edge off the *frisson*
evoked by a creature so disturbing as *The Catipoce*.

> 'O Harry, Harry! hold me close—
>   I fear some animile.
> It is the horny Catipoce
>   With her outrageous smile!'
>
> Thus spoke the maiden in alarm;
>   She had good cause to fear:
> The Catipoce can do great harm,
>   If any come too near.
>
> Despite her looks, do not presume
>   The creature's ways are mild;
> For many have gone mad on whom
>   The Catipoce has smiled.
>
> She lurks in woods at close of day
>   Among the toadstools soft,
> Or sprawls on musty sacks and hay
>   In cellar, barn or loft.
>
> Behind neglected rubbish-dumps
>   At dusk your blood will freeze
> Only to glimpse her horny humps
>   And hear her fatal sneeze.
>
> Run, run! adventurous boy or girl—
>   Run home, and do not pause
> To feel her breath around you curl
>   And tempt her carrion claws.

> Avoid her face, for underneath
> That gentle, fond grimace
> Lie four-and-forty crooked teeth—
> My dears, avoid her face!
>
> 'O Harry, Harry! hold me close,
> And hold me close awhile;
> It is the odious Catipoce
> With her devouring smile!'

The great majority of poems in English are in the iambic rhythm, but sometimes a different movement is called for. *The Grey Horse* is written in a cantering, loosely anapaestic rhythm, which gives it lightness.

> A dappled horse stood at the edge of the meadow,
> He was peaceful and quiet and grey as a shadow.
> Something he seemed to be saying to me,
> As he stood in the shade of the chestnut tree . . .

This is a rhythm in which, as I have said, it is difficult, if not impossible, to be serious.[1]

While most of the poems in a collection for young readers should no doubt be simple in form, part of the pleasure of writing such a collection is the opportunity it gives for experiment and variation in the choice or invention of forms. *Noah* is written in a variation of ballad metre in which a fifth line is added to each stanza.

> Noah was an admiral;
> Never a one but he
> Sailed for forty days and nights
> With wife and children three
> On such a mighty sea . . .

The problem in this case—as indeed in all stanzaic verse—is to construct a series of stanzas in which there is no padding—in

[1] An exception is Thomas Wolfe's moving *Burial of Sir John Moore at Corunna*, but here the solemnity is sustained by varying the anapaests of the main movement with frequent iambuses. 'Not a soldier discharged his farewell shot', for instance, has two anapaests followed by two iambuses.

this case, in which the fifth line of each stanza does not sound as if it were tacked on. The poem continues:

> Under his tempest-battered deck
> This admiral had a zoo;
> And all the creatures in the world,
> He kept them, two by two—
> Ant, hippo, Kangaroo . . .

So far I have considered only examples in which four- or three-stress lines are included. These are far the commonest in verse of a simple kind. Occasionally, however, a longer line is demanded. It was the comparative seriousness, the reminiscent or meditative quality of the experience in *The Castle*, already quoted, that suggested a five-stress iambic line. Here is the second of the two stanzas.

> That night I dreamed how in my castle tower
>   There stood a maid, distracted and forlorn,
> Who wrung her white hands, praying for the sound
>   Of horses' hooves and the deliverer's horn.

I do not think this, reminding us of the solemnity of Gray's *Elegy*, is an ideal metre for children's verse, and I have used it sparingly.

By contrast, I used a two-stress line in *Bobadil*, where an effect of unusual lightness was required, to convey the feeling of this shadowy character.

> Far from far
>   Lives Bobadil
> In a tall house
>   On a tall hill.
>
> Out from the high
>   Top window-sill
> On a clear night
>   Leans Bobadil . . .

Again, this seems to me to be a measure which should be used sparingly, though it is useful for the sake of variety.

There is an Irish suggestion in the verse-form of *The Summer Party*, in which two rhymed two-stress lines alternate with a four-stress line: this pattern is repeated, the sixth line rhyming with the third.

> In a blue, blue bonnet
> With posies on it
> Came Mrs Muckle
> To the summer party.
>
> With tight, bright boots on
> And festive suits on
> Came Mr Hearty
> And old Dr Hearty . . .

It may be noted that all the rhymes are feminine—that is, trochaic ('bonnet, on it' and so on). This gives the impression of lightness, gaiety and bustle, adding necessarily to the speed of the lines. Readers of Francis Mahoney's *The Bells of Shandon* will recall that the repeated trochaic rhymes there add a note of wistful nostalgia.

A verse form somewhat more elaborate in appearance is that of *Avalon*.

> In Avalon lies Arthur yonder;
> Over his head the planets wander.
> A great King
> And a great King was he . . .

If the last two lines are run together, it will be seen that, like the two previous lines, they form a three-stress line. Breaking them up in this way imposes on the reading a certain slowness or deliberation, and this adds solemnity, as does the repetition:

> . . . A great King
> And a great King . . .

The poem concludes:

> . . . By his side sleeps Guinevere;
> Of ladies she had no peer.
> A fair Queen
> And a fair Queen was she.

At midnight comes Jack the Knave
By moonlight to rob their grave.
　　A false boy
　　And a false boy is he.

Jewels he takes, and rings,
The gift of nobles and kings—
　　Bright things,
　　O bright things to see!

On harvest-field and town
The moon and stars look down.
Centuries without number
King and Queen are a-slumber.
　　Long have they lain.
In time they will rise again
And all false knaves be slain.
Once more Arthur shall reign.
　　A great King
　　And a great King is he.

Pat's Fiddle is written in a still more elaborate verse form.
A seven-line stanza is succeeded by a four-line refrain.

When Pat plays his fiddle
　　In the great empty hall,
And the flame of each candle
　　Is shiny and small,
　　　　Then to hear the brave jingle,
　　　　Oh, how my feet tingle
And how I do wish we could have a fine ball!

　　　Like a riddle, like a riddle
　　　　Without any answer,
　　　Is a fiddle, sweet fiddle,
　　　　With never a dancer . . .

The dancing, song-like movement is enhanced by the echoing
repetitions ('fiddle, sweet fiddle', etc.) and by the combination
of iambuses and lilting dactyls and anapaests. This may be too

D

elaborate for young readers to read aloud without practice, but provided the mind is kept on the meaning, it should not be difficult to stress the lines correctly and read them without tripping up. Indeed, an important aim in writing verse for children—or anyone else, for that matter—is to achieve an appeal to the ear without encouraging a monotonous singsong either in silent or in spoken reading. In short, the aim is to keep a balance between metrical regularity and rhythmical irregularity. The kind of verse I have written for children attempts to have this in common with good traditional folk-song: that is is based on the rhythms of speech. It should be read always with an ear for the sense, not as a mechanical jingle. The latter effect is often produced by reading it too fast. A poem should impose its own natural speed and rhythm. If the reader trips over a line, he is probably reading too fast.

Islands, the 'I' poem of the alphabet series, *Ragged Robin*, is written in semi-irregular form, combining lines of different lengths, most having either four or five stresses. It begins with a group of three lines, of which the first has three stresses, the other two four each.

> I, with my mind's eye, see
> Islands and indies fair and free,
> Fair and far in the coral sea . . .

Then follows a group of seven lines, which lengthen as the poem proceeds.

> Out of the sea rise palmy shores;
> Out of the shore rise plumy trees;
> Out of each tree a feathered bird
> Sings with a voice like which no voice was ever heard,
> And palm and plume and feather
> Blend and bloom together
> In colours like the green of summer weather . . .

The intention of this irregular and apparently arbitrary pattern was to convey a mood of dreamy repose, the daydreaming of

pure wishful fantasy. The mood is continued in a final group
of six lines:

> And in this island scene
> There is no clash nor quarrel;
> Here the seas wash
> In shining fields of coral
> Indies and isles that lie
> Deep in my mind's eye.

Is this perhaps too sophisticated for children? It should be
mentioned that *Ragged Robin*, more than any other of my books
of verse, was conceived as a picture book, and in some cases,
therefore, the words are subordinate to the illustrations. The
words of *Islands* and the delicate and evocative coloured illustrations by Jane Paton are complementary.

Brand is a frankly Anglo-Saxon exercise in vigorous alliterative verse.

> Brand the Blacksmith with his hard hammer
> Beats out shoes for the hooves of horses.
> Bagot the Boy works at the bellows
> To make fine mounts for the King's forces.
>
> Better the music than bell or bugle
> When 'Huff!' go the bellows and 'Ding!' goes the hammer.
> 'Better this work by far,' says Bagot,
> 'Than banging of school bell and grinding at grammar.'

Kay, already quoted, is another Arthurian poem, in places
resembling a tongue-twister.

> . . . This is the Keep,
> And this is the key.
> Who keeps the key
> Of the Keep?
>> Sir Kay.

I have been illustrating the variety of metrical and rhythmic
patterns employed in many of my children's poems. They range
from the regularity of ballad metre to some of the free forms

I have just been quoting. The ability of children, or anyone else, to read the freer forms effectively depends on their capacity to get away from the singsong sometimes used in reading regular metrical lines. Crucial to their success here is the matter of speed. On the whole there is a tendency to read all verse too fast, especially if the reader is nervous, unrelaxed or not sufficiently familiar with the text. Each poem, by its thought or content, should dictate its own speed. A poem, however 'musical' in sound, should always be read for the sense. *Islands*, for instance, quoted earlier, demands a slow, meditative tempo. *Brand* could with advantage be read faster, and with strong rhythmical emphasis, and a vigorous attack where the alliterative consonants occur. In my opinion the most satisfactory poems for children are those with an underlying metrical pattern with considerable rhythmic variation.

Little Fan

'I don't like the look of little Fan, mother,
    I don't like her looks a little bit.
Her face—well, it's not exactly different,
    But there's something wrong with it.

'She went down to the sea-shore yesterday,
    And she talked to somebody there,
Now she won't do anything but sit
    And comb out her yellowy hair.

'Her eyes are shiny and she sings, mother,
    Like nobody ever sang before.
Perhaps they gave her something queer to eat,
    Down by the rocks on the shore.

'Speak to me, speak, little Fan dear,
    Aren't you feeling very well?
Where have you been and what are you singing,
    And what's that seaweedy smell?

'Where did you get that shiny comb love,
  And those pretty coral beads so red?
Yesterday you had two legs, I'm certain,
  But now there's something else instead.

'I don't like the looks of little Fan, mother,
  You'd best go and close the door.
Watch now, or she'll be gone for ever
  To the rocks by the brown sandy shore.'

The metrical pattern is a simple one: four-stress and three-stress lines alternate, but it would be hard to analyse the lines according to any set pattern of feet. The rhythm, in fact, approximates to that of speech, and this is appropriate in what is meant to be an address by a child, perhaps an elder sister of Little Fan, to her mother. Some of the lines, separated from their context, could indeed be prose speech. 'I don't like her looks a little bit.'

I have not experimented with entirely free—that is, ametrical and unrhymed—verse for children, though the form has possibilities. It is, some writers think, harder to compose than metrical verse, though children themselves do write excellent free verse. My very first poem written especially for young readers was in fact a piece of rhymed free verse, a sort of extended metaphor in which the sea is described as if it were a large, shaggy dog. The poem begins:

The Sea

The sea is a hungry dog,
Giant and grey.
He rolls on the beach all day.
With his clashing teeth and shaggy jaws

Hour upon hour he gnaws
The rumbling, tumbling stones,
And 'Bones, bones, bones, bones'
The giant sea-dog moans,
Licking his greasy paws . . .

And when the night wind roars
And the moon rocks in the stormy cloud,
He bounds to his feet and snuffs and sniffs,
Shaking his wet sides over the cliffs,
And howls and hollos long and loud . . .

The language here is chosen to sound rough and boisterous.
The conclusion of the poem is in contrast. There is a complete
change of mood and key.

But on quiet days in May or June,
When even the grasses on the dune
Play no more their reedy tune,
With his head between his paws
He lies on the sandy shores,
So quiet, so quiet, he scarcely snores.

CHAPTER 8

DICTION

BY 'DICTION' is meant the detailed choice of words and phrases. In poems for children I have always aimed at a simple, clear, graphic diction, though without making the mistaken attempt to choose only words that are likely to be familiar already to potential readers. Without labouring a point with which all those with any discrimination in the matter are familiar, I would emphasize that the false simplicity known as 'writing down' to children is quite out of place. If a child meets a word whose meaning he does not know, he will do one of two things: ignore it and be satisfied with a general understanding of its context; or find out what it means by asking or by looking it up. Not to 'stretch' a child's understanding by enlarging his vocabulary is to evade a responsibility and invite boredom. Clarity and concreteness of diction are also a requisite of verse that is to make any impact and create a lasting impression.

I will here recall the first two stanzas of *The Wandering Moon*, quoted earlier.

> Age after age and all alone,
>   She turns through endless space,
> Showing the watchers on the earth
>   Her round and rocky face.
> Enchantment comes upon all hearts
>   That feel her lonely grace.
>
> Mount Newton is the highest peak
>   Upon the wandering moon,
> And there perhaps the witches dance
>   To some fantastic tune,

> And in the half-light cold and grey
> Their incantations croon . . .

By 'clear' I do not mean 'easily definable'. 'Age after age' is a
generalized expression indicating the passage of immense tracts
of time. Epithets should be used sparingly and with as much
precision as possible. An excess of epithets detracts from the
hard concreteness of a description. 'Endless', 'round and rocky',
'lonely', 'fantastic', 'cold and grey'—some may feel that there
are too many of these descriptive adjectives. The aim is to use
enough to create the mood and atmosphere needed, but not so
many as to amount to mere padding.

'The half-light cold and grey' and 'Their incantations croon'
are examples of something which, if overdone, amounts to
a fault: inversion of the natural syntactical order of English
speech. Such inversions are usually caused by one of two ne-
cessities—that of getting the rhythm right and that of fulfilling
the chosen rhyme-pattern. Some writers would have straight-
ened out the fifth line of stanza two and made it: 'And in the
cold and grey half-light'. It is a matter of taste. As for the last
line, I would defend the inversion on the ground that 'croon' is
a strong word on which to end the stanza.

A device often used effectively in English verse is that of
assonance, or near-rhyme. English, being an uninflected language, is comparatively hard up for rhymes. Italian, by contrast,
is almost too rich in them.

The Grey Horse

> A dappled horse stood at the edge of the meadow,
> He was peaceful and quiet and grey as a shadow.
> Something he seemed to be saying to me,
> As he stood in the shade of the chestnut tree.

> 'It's a wonderful morning,' he seemed to say,
> 'So jump on my back, and let's be away!
> It's over the hedge we'll leap and fly,
> And up the hill to the edge of the sky.

'For over the hill there are fields without end;
On the galloping downs we can run like the wind.
Down pathways we'll canter, by streams we'll stray,
Oh, jump on my back and let's be away!'

As I went by the meadow one fine summer morn,
The grey horse had gone like a ghost with the dawn;
He had gone like a ghost and not waited for me,
And it's over the hilltop he'd surely be.

These rhymed couplets contain three near-rhymes—'meadow' and 'shadow', 'end' and 'wind', 'morn' and 'dawn'. Purists used to call the last example a 'cockney' rhyme, and no doubt it would be offensive to a good Scots ear: I would avoid it wherever possible. But it will pass in a context where assonance is evident.

Some of the poems in my volumes of children's verse might more properly be called 'rhymes'. If there is a distinction between a rhyme and other kinds of verse, it might be that the rhymes in it dictate the course of the poem more than does the meaning. It should always be a poet's aim, when employing rhyme, that the rhyme should appear to come spontaneously and neither dictate the meaning nor seem to be merely subservient to it. In other words, a poet's instinctive flair for choosing the right word will include, not only its meaning and its rhythm, but also its sound, or that part of its sound that determines its quality as a rhyming word.

Doctor John Hearty, though old as a fossil,
Could dance like a fairy and sing like a throstle . . .

Why 'fossil'? Because it is a fitting image of extreme old age—an exaggeration, clearly. Why 'throstle'? Because it rhymes nearly enough, with 'fossil' and denotes a bird remarkable for its singing. The rhyme combination has the advantage that it is uncommon. The lines might have been, say:

Doctor John Hearty, though old as a mountain,
Could sing like a throstle and run like a fountain.

This would have exemplified something we should all try to avoid, but are obliged to use on occasions—the well-worn rhyme. 'Mountain' and 'fountain' is one of the most jaded rhymes in English.

The little tristich *Others* came into my head quite spontaneously. It is a jingle, but has the freshness of a traditional rhyme.

> 'Mother, oh mother! where shall we hide us?
> Others there are in the house beside us—
> Moths and mice and crooked brown spiders!'

Here are the first few lines of *Mick*, of which the opening couplet was also dictated by an unusual rhyme—or rather, near-rhyme.

> Mick my mongrel-O
> Lives in a bungalow,
> Painted green with a round doorway.
> With an eye for cats
> And a nose for rats
> He lies on his threshold half the day . . .

The 'O' suffixed to 'mongrel' is in a folk tradition, in which near-rhymes, or 'off rhymes', play a considerable part. I have illustrated this previously by referring to the popular children's game of 'Oranges and Lemons'. Such near-rhymes, or 'off rhymes', I admit, fascinate me as much as when I began a poem quoted earlier,

> The old King of Dorchester,
> He had a little orchestra.

The fascination of such off-rhymes comes partly from the speculation as to which came first in the writer's mind, 'orchestra' or 'Dorchester'.

W

> The King sent for his wise men all
> To find a rhyme for W;

> When they had thought a good long time
> But could not think of a single rhyme,
> 'I'm sorry,' said he, 'to trouble you.'

This perhaps is the *reductio ad absurdum* of the whole game. It is a rhyme about rhyming. The writer, as it were, pats himself on the back for being, in company with the King, cleverer than all the wise men.

Ideally, as I have indicated earlier, the word-order in a poem, unless there is some special reason why it should not be so, follows the natural prose order. In this way clarity of meaning is maintained. Sometimes, however, the exigencies of the rhyme-scheme makes this impossible. Here is the first stanza of *The Toadstool Wood*:

> The toadstool wood is dark and mouldy,
>   And has a ferny smell.
> About the trees hangs something quiet
>   And queer—like a spell.

All is well until line 3: 'About the trees hangs something quiet . . .' The prose order of this and the succeeding line would be: 'Something quiet and queer, like a spell, hangs about the trees.' Of course this order is not permitted by the rhyme and rhythm. I think it is possible to justify the inversion on the ground that it throws emphasis on the word 'quiet'. The prose order is flatter. The poem continues:

> Beneath the arching sprays of bramble
>   Small creatures make their holes;
> Over the moss's close green velvet
>   The stilted spider strolls.

The inversion in the first line ('Beneath the arching sprays . . .') would be perfectly in order even in prose. The same is true of line 3 ('Over the moss's . . .'). Stanza 3 runs:

> The stalks of toadstools pale and slender
>   That grow from that old log,
> Bars they might be to imprison
>   A prince turned to a frog.

Here the inversion is very marked. I would not care to defend this against a purist who considered 'bars they might be . . .' clumsy. I found the inversion, however, unavoidable but worth tolerating for the sake of the metaphor. But I admit the picture is very fanciful. The final stanza, I hope, does something to restore regularity in word order.

> There lives no mumbling witch nor wizard
>   In this uncanny place,
> Yet you might think you saw at twilight
>   A little, crafty face.

Mrs Button is intended as a sympathetic portrait of an old woman who sweeps out the church on weekdays. She has trouble with her feet—those feet by which everyone who has to do a lot of standing is aroused, sooner or later, to self-pity. It seemed appropriate, therefore, that the phrase 'poor feet' should be used as a refrain.

> When Mrs Button, of a morning,
>   Comes creaking down the street,
> You hear her old two black boots whisper
>   'Poor feet—poor feet—poor feet!'
>
> When Mrs Button, every Monday,
>   Sweeps the chapel neat,
> All down the long, hushed aisles they whisper
>   'Poor feet—poor feet—poor feet!'
>
> Mrs Button after dinner
>   (It is her Sunday treat)
> Sits down and takes her two black boots off
>   And rests her two poor feet.

Something will be said later about onomatopoeia: in passing, it should be noted that the triple repetition of the phrase is intended to echo the sense, suggesting perhaps that the cleaner's exertions have given her something of a limp.

A thematic rhyme occurs also in *Old Moll*, which uses one rhyme throughout, until the very last line.

The moon is up,
  The night owls scritch.
Who's that croaking?
  The frog in the ditch.
Who's that howling?
  The old hound bitch.
My neck tingles,
  My elbows itch,
My hair rises,
  My eyelids twitch.
What's in that pot
  So rare and rich?
Who's that crouching
  In a cloak like pitch?
Hush! that's Old Moll—
  They say she's a
Most ree-markable old party.

Of course the final arhythmic phrase is a deliberate avoiding of
the dreaded word which, by now, the successive 'itch' rhymes
have led the reader to expect. Is the device too contrived? The
answer, I think, is no, provided the poem is read aloud effectively—that is, with a pause before the final phrase and an awe-
inspiring hush in the voice. Whether or not this will cause a
willing suspension of disbelief in the existence of witches I do
not know.

Something more should be said about adjectives and nouns.
Atmosphere can be created by the use of descriptive adjectives
or epithets. But strength, concreteness and graphic quality are
gained by avoiding adjectives and concentrating on nouns. A
poem can indeed be made from a list of nouns and very little
else besides. *Little Minnie Mystery* (already referred to) is an
account of a hoarder. Many, perhaps most, children go through
a hoarding stage. It is unnecessary to enumerate the treasures
they amass. Minnie Mystery is a lady who has never outgrown
the habit.

Little Minnie Mystery has packets and parcels
  All tied about with laces and strings,

And all full of scraps and patches and morsels
    And oddments and pieces and bits of things.

All tied about with strings and laces
    Are old Minnie Mystery's wonderful stores,
And she stows them away in all sorts of places—
    Cupboards and cases and chests of drawers.

All day long you will hear her caper
    From attic to basement, up and down stairs,
Rummaging and rustling with tissue paper
    And rattling keys and climbing on chairs.

What does she keep in her parcels and packets?—
    Why, buckles and beads and knobs and handles,
Playing-cards, curtain-rings, loops, and lockets,
    Letters and labels and Christmas-tree candles,

And a seashell box and a peacock feather
    And a picture postcard from Tonypandy—
Everything neat and fastened together,
    All that could possibly come in handy.

'Waste not, want not,' says Minnie Mystery.
    'Everything's sure to come in some day.'
So, although she should live to the end of history,
    Nothing she ever will throw away.

This contains no more than two strictly descriptive adjectives, 'wonderful' and 'neat'. The verbs, too, are few. The only significant ones are 'stows', 'caper', 'rustling', 'rummaging', 'climbing'—a fair account of Minnie's activities. As for the catalogue of nouns: first, there are the general names for the places in which she keeps her stores—'packets', 'parcels', 'cupboards and cases'; then a few generalized kinds of treasure— 'scraps', 'morsels', 'oddments', 'bits'. But the centre of the poem is the particularized list of treasures that gives it its credibility, its actuality, from 'buckles and beads' to the

'picture postcard from Tonypandy'; and it is a fact not easy
to explain that the more particular such a catalogue is, the
more convincing it is. 'Why Tonypandy?' the reader may
wonder. No doubt Minnie had a Welsh cousin—useful, because rhymes for 'handy' are scarce. Apart from the rhymes,
however, the list has to be assembled with care. It has to sound,
as well as look, convincing. It has to run smoothly off the
tongue, in order to give a feeling of unity to something so
random and arbitrary. To this end alliteration has been
called into service—'buckles and beads', 'loops and lockets',
'letters and labels', 'picture postcard'. Too much alliteration
would make the list sound contrived and artificial. A few but
not too many rarer or more outlandish articles are included—
'a seashell box and a peacock feather'. So the picture is built up
to cohere and convince.

Mr Bellairs, already quoted, depends mainly on nouns for its
effect, but it will serve again as an example where a few adjectives and adverbs have been used carefully, especially at the
beginning, to heighten the atmosphere.

> In a huge hoary mansion
>   Lives Mr Bellairs,
> With four or five storeys
>   And hundreds of stairs.
>
> The gates of his garden
>   Are made of wrought iron,
> From the top of each gatepost
>   Glares down a great lion.
>
> The trees in the garden
>   Are ancient and stately,
> And high in their branches
>   Rooks mumble sedately.
>
> The tails of the peacocks
>   Sweep by on the grass;
> The fish in the fishpond
>   Gleam gold as they pass.

Superior tulips
Adorn the parterres
In the exquisite garden
Of Mr Bellairs . . .

Here the words 'huge' and 'hoary', 'ancient and stately', 'sedately', 'superior' and 'exquisite' combine to convey the atmosphere. It is easy but mistaken to pile up epithets. They must be selected judiciously and not appear superfluous.

Let me refer once again to the introductory poem to *Prefabulous Animiles*. After the mainly substantival list of everyday animals the poem goes on:

. . . Let no one suppose that creatures like those
Are ALL that the Animal Kingdom can show:

NO!

When the woods rumble low
And storm clouds ride by in the purplish sky,
At the corners of dreams,
Round the edges of sleep,
There's a something that *seems* to be going to creep,
To crawl or to climb, to lumber or leap
Round the corners of dreams and the edges of sleep.
You cannot be sure that you fastened the door,
You cannot be certain that under the curtain
There isn't a tail or a paw or a claw.
And what makes you wonder is never the thunder
Nor wind in the chimney nor rain on the tiles,
It *must* be—
PREFABULOUS ANIMILES!
So if any suppose
That the creatures he knows
In pond or in park,
By daylight and dark,
Are all that the Animal Kingdom contains,
Then some day he'll see them lurking in lanes,
Or breaking down hedges and fences and stiles—
He'll *see* the Prefabulous Animiles.

This again depends for its effect mainly on nouns unadorned with epithets. Indeed, 'purplish' is the only significant one in the whole quotation. But there is a significant accumulation of verbs, which activate the otherwise static picture—'creep', 'crawl', 'climb', 'lumber', 'leap', 'lurk'.

The temptation to a resourceful writer to go beyond the bounds of conventional language and use words on or beyond the fringe of conventional vocabulary is considerable. Neologisms go back at least as far as Lear and Carroll, indeed much further. These two were the first to use them in poems especially written for, or read by, children. There are two kinds of neologism: the wholly obscure and the reasonably obvious. Carroll's 'slithy toves' and 'mome raths' would be incomprehensible but for the key to their meaning that their inventor supplied. A plausible guess may be made at the meaning of his 'O frabjous day!' This is a useful way of increasing the resources of language. At least one word invented by Carroll has passed into the language: 'chortle', a combination of 'chuckle' and 'snort'.

The lines I wrote under the title *Grim and Gloomy* employ a number of devices, such as alliteration and double rhymes, including neologisms of the second, more reasonable type:

> Oh, grim and gloomy,
> So grim and gloomy
> Are the caves beneath the sea.
> Oh, rare but roomy
> And bare and boomy,
> Those salt sea caverns be.
>
> Oh, slim and slimy
> Or grey and grimy
> Are the animals of the sea.
> Salt and oozy
> And safe and snoozy
> The caves where those animals be.

Hark to the shuffling,
Huge and snuffling,
Ravenous, cavernous, great sea-beasts!
But fair and fabulous,
Tintinnabulous,
Gay and fabulous are their feasts.

Ah, but the queen of the sea,
The querulous, perilous sea!
How the curls of her tresses
The pearls on her dresses,
Sway and swirl in the waves,
How cosy and dozy,
How sweet ring-a-rosy
Her bower in the deep-sea caves!

Oh, rare but roomy
And bare and boomy
Those caverns under the sea,
And grave and grandiose,
Safe and sandiose
The dens of her denizens be.

The only word whose meaning children might find it hard to guess is 'tintinnabulous', but a look at the dictionary is all that is necessary. When I wrote the poem, I thought I had invented this word, but I found later that it was used as early as 1791. It means 'tinkling in a bell-like manner'. The other unusual words—'boomy', 'snoozy', 'dozy', 'ring-a-rosy', 'sandiose'—are, so to speak, words that ought to exist if they do not.

Much more extreme explorations into the pleasures and temptations of neologism occur in *Prefabulous Animiles*. Here is the beginning of *The Osc*.

This is the superfluminous Osc,
A mild and serious liver,
He skims each day from dawn till dusk
The surface of the river.

> For gentleness he is the best
> Of all amphibious creatures;
> His wide and wondering eyes suggest
> An old, forgotten teacher's.
>
> In, out—in, out—he weaves his way
> Along the limpid shallows,
> Or upside-down hangs half a day
> Amidst the ruminous sallows . . .

'Superfluminous' is difficult for any without Latin. No doubt it was suggested to me by a recollection of the Latin title of one of the Psalms in the Anglican Prayer Book: 'Super flumina Babylonis'—'By the waters of Babylon'. But it seemed to me a useful word, worthy to exist. As for 'ruminous', that cannot be difficult. It must mean something like 'murmuring'. The 'fexious beast' in *The Blether* and 'joysome odes' in *The Nonny* are easy enough in their context; 'multitudinivorous' in *The Chickamungus* is a more obscure coinage, and the 'half-grown formicoots' on which this creature feeds must be left to the imagination.

The essence of inventing neologisms is, I think, that they should sound natural, unforced, almost inevitable. They should sound like words whose non-existence hitherto was more accident than design.

Puns should be used sparingly, but sometimes one is in the mood for them. The simple word-game played in *The Song of the Dumb Waiter* is that of taking literally the names of half a dozen objects used metaphorically—'flower-bed', 'boot-tree', and so on.

> Who went to sleep in the flower-bed?
> Who let the fire-dog out of the shed?
>
> Who sailed the sauce-boat down the stream?
> What did the railway-sleeper dream?
>
> Who was it chopped the boot-tree down,
> And rode the clothes-horse through the town?

Mrs Golightly is a fantasy which sprang entirely from a fascination with the name and its possibilities in conjunction with that bizarre, classically comic object, the golosh. This useful article of footwear I supposed to be Edwardian, or at the earliest Victorian, until recourse to the dictionary informed me that its first appearance in English literature was no later than Chaucer. In his time the 'galoche' was 'a patten or clog', not of course the rubber overshoe intended in my poem.

> Mrs Golightly's goloshes
> Are roomy and large;
> Through water she slithers and sloshes,
> As safe as a barge.
>
> When others at home must be stopping,
> To market she goes,
> And returns later on with her shopping
> Tucked into her toes.

One of the essentials of children's verse is that it should stimulate an interest in words for their own sake. Word-games are a natural activity of civilised and literate people. But a game does not always entail jokes. The game of letting one's mind play on the associations of a single adjective can produce such a poem as *Grey*.

> Grey is the sky, and grey the woodman's cot
> With grey smoke tumbling from the chimney-pot.
> The flagstones are grey that lead to the door;
> Grey is the hearth, and grey the worn old floor.
>
> The old man by the fire nods in his chair;
> Grey are his clothes and silvery grey his hair.
> Grey are the shadows around him creeping,
> And grey the mouse from the corner peeping.

Out of a picture emerges what is almost a story. Quite a different story is suggested by the perhaps unpromising title *Waiting*.

Waiting, waiting, waiting
   For the party to begin;
Waiting, waiting, waiting
   For the laughter and din;
Waiting, waiting, waiting
   With hair just so
And clothes trim and tidy
   From top-knot to toe.
The floor is all shiny,
   The lights are ablaze;
There are sweetmeats in plenty
   And cakes beyond praise.
Oh the games and dancing,
   The tricks and the toys,
The music and the madness
   The colour and noise!
Waiting, waiting, waiting
For the first knock on the door—
Was ever such waiting,
   Such waiting before?

The effect of repetition here is to increase the feeling of suspense. Indeed, the lines are simply a brief essay on the impatience of a child.

The effort to get children to appreciate words for their own sake, their sound, feel and flavour, leads to experiments in repetition, like *Waiting*. But whereas the purpose in those lines is to create suspense, in *Mermaid Song* the aim is different. As the title implies, this is a poem in which music is more important than meaning. The ear is invited, by the frequent repetitions, to dwell on the sound-quality of the words. I will quote these lines once more.

She sits by the sea in the clear, shining air,
   And the sailors call her Moonlight, Moonlight;
They see her smoothing her wavy hair,
   And they hear her singing, singing.
The sea-shells learn their tunes from her

And the big fish listen with never a stir
  To catch the voice of Moonlight, Moonlight,
And I would hark for a year and a year
  To hear her singing, singing.

As I said earlier, dialect should be used only sparingly except perhaps in a case where a whole poem is an exercise in
dialect, which might be another legitimate way of getting
children to think about language. This exercise has never appealed to me, but I see no reason why it should not be successful.
But the trouble with dialect written by a literary person is that
it can degenerate into a means of being patronizing at the
expense of less-educated people, a mere music-hall laugh-
raising device. Good dialect poems have been written by Scots
poets, writers of Cockney ballads and by the Dorset parson,
William Barnes. Less successful are Tennyson's experiments in
dialect poems, probably because you are aware, as you are not
with Barnes, of the self-consciousness of a professional literary
man. You are unlikely to persuade children, as distinct from
adults, to smile at rustic or town speech unless it happens to be
your own natural way of speaking.

Slang is another matter. The use of slang in poetry, especially
perhaps for children, does not appeal to me, and I cannot write
in a way which does not appeal to me. It is the fashion to regard
anything suggestive of a need for restraint as 'square', but I
think that enough slang is used in everyday life to make it
unnecessary to introduce it freely into verse. The trouble with
slang and colloquialism is twofold: first, it is often an imprecise
and lazy way of speaking; secondly, it goes out of fashion and
is in constant need of renewal. Many words that were formerly
colloquialisms have of course passed into, and so extended, the
language; but many more are mere vogue words, substitutes
for others just as expressive, and destined to pass speedily out
of usage. Here are the opening and closing stanzas of *My
Singing Aunt*. Readers must judge for themselves whether the
use of 'barmy' is permissible. (Admittedly the word has been

officially regarded as standard English for well over a century,
but most would still consider it to be slang.)

> The voice of magic melody
>   With which my aunt delights me,
> It drove my uncle to the grave
>   And now his ghost affrights me.
> This was the song she used to sing
>   When I could scarcely prattle,
> And as her top notes rose and fell
>   They made the sideboard rattle . . .
>
> Thus sang my aunt in days gone by
>   To soothe, caress, and calm me;
> But what delighted me so much
>   Drove her poor husband barmy.
> So now when past the church I stray,
>   'Tis not the night-wind moaning,
> That chills my blood and stops my breath,
>   But poor old uncle's groaning.

Ultimately a poet's diction is a matter for his personal tastes
and standards. If his tastes are common-place and his standards
low, they will be reflected unmistakably in his verse. He should
aim at a diction which is neither too literary or pedantic on the
one hand, nor too imprecise and sloppy on the other. It should
be harmonious without being soporific; it should be easy and
natural, respecting the standards of good speech, but willing
to try out the resources of the unusual, the out-of-the-way. No
single rule can govern a poet's diction. The resources of English
are virtually unlimited; unlimited, therefore, the opportunities
for the poet. He has never finished selecting and discarding, and,
the more exacting his ideal, the less likely he is ever to be
satisfied.

CHAPTER 9

FIGURES OF SPEECH

To READERS with memories of examinations in English grammar the heading 'Figures of Speech' may have a depressing look. However discredited formal grammar lessons are in some quarters, we do use figures of speech; indeed, a developed language is inconceivable without them. Certainly there could be little poetry except of the simplest possible character. If, then, the study of figures of speech in the abstract is dry, they may nevertheless be discussed fruitfully in a context of poetic illustrations.

Of all the figures that add most to poetry and extend the language, simile and metaphor are the most common and the most valuable. A simile, usually involving the words 'like' or 'as', is a comparison: some writers distinguish between comparison and simile proper, but the distinction is not relevant here. A metaphor is in essence a compressed simile. 'Food prices rocketed' is a snappier way of saying 'Food prices rose as rapidly and spectacularly as a rocket rises into the air'. Metaphor is liable to occur wherever anything is referred to otherwise than in a stictly literal sense. The word 'rose' in the example just quoted is in itself metaphorical. We may say that prises *rise*, because they become higher. But is not 'high' also a metaphor? How, in any literal sense, can it be said that the figure 7 is higher than 5? How can it be said that the note G is higher than F? The answer must be that such a use of words like 'high' and 'low' is conventional, and that such metaphorical usages are in the very fabric of our language. 'Fabric' again is a metaphor. But it is a dead metaphor: we do not, in using it as I have just used it, consciously imagine a piece of woven material. Dead metaphors are to be avoided in poetry with at

least as much care as new or living metaphors are to be
sought.

> At sunset, when the night-dews fall,
> Out of the ivy on the wall
> With horns outstretched and pointed tail
> Comes the grey and noiseless snail.
> On ivy stems she clambers down,
> Carrying her house of brown.
> Safe in the dark, no greedy eye
> Can her tender body spy,
> While she herself, a hungry thief,
> Searches out the freshest leaf.
> She travels on as best she can
> Like a toppling caravan.

As far as line 6 this is straightforward, literal description. In
line 6 occurs the simple metaphor 'house' for 'shell'. Strictly
speaking the word 'thief' is a metaphor, but from the gardener's
point of view it is literal enough. The last line is a simile; the
'house' has become a 'toppling caravan'. The purpose of this
comparison is to convey the top-heavy, slow and trundling
gait of a fully grown snail. It might be objected that the difference in size between a snail and a caravan is too extreme. I did
in fact consider the metaphorical alternative to the last line, 'A
small and toppling caravan.' In the end I thought it better to
leave the adjustment in scale to the reader's imagination. Even
'small' is perhaps not small enough, and 'A tiny, toppling
caravan' was also rejected. After all, a fully grown snail, such
I was picturing, is big by snail—and child—standards.

A simile may heighten an effect by recalling something
familiar, or by inviting the imagination to dwell on something
it has never seen. The strange may be made familiar or the
familiar invested with strangeness. As an illustration I quote
once more the short poem *Shiny*.

> Shiny are the chestnut leaves
> Before they unfold.

> The inside of a buttercup
>   Is like polished gold.
> A pool in the sunshine
>   Is bright too,
> And a fine silver shilling
>   When it is new.
> But the round, full moon,
>   So clear and white,
> How brightly she shines
>   On a winter night!
> Slowly she rises,
>   Higher and higher,
> With a cold clear light
>   Like ice on fire.

The comparison between a buttercup and polished gold is between two familiar but different objects. But the comparison of the moon to 'ice on fire' introduces something no one has seen, and the conclusion suggested is that, *if* one could see ice on fire, it would look like the full moon on a clear, cold night.

A simple way of keeping the language of a poem alive is the deliberate avoidance of a stereotyped comparison in favour of an unusual one. Here are stanzas 2 and 4 of *The Old Wife and the Ghost*, already quoted in another context.

> . . . About that kitchen neat and clean
>   The ghost goes pottering round.
> But the poor old wife is deaf as a boot
>   And so hears never a sound . . .
>
> He blows on his hands to make them warm,
>   And whistles aloud 'Whee—hee!'
> But still as a sack the old soul lies
>   And never a sound hears she.

The first cliché that comes to mind as a simile for deafness is of course 'post', but the substitution of 'boot' invites the reader to pause and reflect whether it is a just simile. The same is true of 'still as a sack', instead of 'a stone'. I don't claim that this is more than a simple device, but so deadening is the use of clichés that their avoidance can be a positive, not a merely negative, duty on the part of a writer.

> You'd say it was a wedding,
>   So glib and gay the talk is,
> When old Mr Dorkis
>   Goes out with Mrs Dorkis.
>
> Of horses, carts, carriages,
> Birthdays and marriages,
> Of old friends and foes,
> Of windfalls and woes,
> Of bad luck and good luck
> With cow, calf, chicken or duck—
> Of such is their talk
> When they go for a walk.
>
> As many are the jokes
>   Of old Mr Dorkis
> As a wheel has spokes
>   Or a pig porkers.

This is nothing more than an extended comparison—a comparison between the conversation of two jolly people and the gaiety of a wedding. The final four lines contain two similes that avoid the obvious. Anyone who objects that a wheel does not have many spokes must be referred to the wheel of a bicycle.

Here once again are the last six lines of *Under Ground*.

> . . . Downward the branching tree-roots spread
> Into the country of the dead.
>
> Deep down, the buried rocks and stones
> Are like the earth's gigantic bones.
>
> In the dark kingdom under ground
> How many marvellous things are found!

This poem, it may be remembered, is an exploration of the depths of the earth from the surface downwards. 'The country of the dead' has metaphorical overtones suggestive of primitive cosmology. When the exploration goes deeper, the metaphor changes from cosmology to physiology. A comparison is made between the rocky substrata of the earth and its supposed 'bones'. Perhaps this is a metaphysical conceit rather than a true metaphor, but it may appeal to the thoughful reader.

The first two stanzas of *Mrs Farleigh-Fashion* contain several similes, which present this sartorial prima donna in two different lights.

> Mrs Farleigh-Fashion
> Flies into a passion
> If any other frock is finer than hers.
> How she bobs and bounces
> In her fleecy flounces,
> She's like a queen in her feathers and furs.
>
> She has a gown of flame,
> Which puts ours to shame,
> And one that billows like the boisterous sea.
> She has another of silk,
> White as morning milk,
> That sighs and whispers like wind in a tree . . .

The comparison of Mrs Farleigh-Fashion to a 'queen' is obvious enough and points to the lady's hauteur and social ambition. But the similes in the second stanza present the other side of the picture. The metaphor 'flame' is of course a common name for a certain colour, but the suggestion of movement makes the picture a little more alive than would a mere colour adjective. Another of Mrs Farleigh-Fashion's creations is of a billowing blue-green material 'like the boisterous sea'; yet another is of white silk 'that sighs and whispers like wind in a tree'. Such images are intended to convey the poetic, the sensuously pleasing aspect of *haute couture*. We can all delight in the sight of beautiful clothes without being repelled by the vanity that often goes with them.

Sometimes a simile may be used, not in order to describe an unfamiliar object (say, one of Mrs Farleigh-Fashion's dresses) by evoking something familiar (morning milk or the foaming sea), but in order to bring together two equally familiar or unfamiliar things. The purpose is not so much descriptive as evocative, romantically suggestive.

> A stream far off beneath the moon
> Flowed silver-bright and thin,
> Winding its way like some slow tune
> Played on a violin . . .

If the reader's mental picture of a lowland stream in the moonlight is stronger than his aural image of a violin tune, he may thereby add to his musical experience; it may not have occurred to him that a melody can wind and linger and return upon itself in this way. If he has a good musical memory, a good inner ear, but has not seen a stream by moonlight, then his visual sense will be reinforced by his feeling for music. In either case, the two images, linked together in a simile, reinforce each other and contribute to the romantic atmosphere that the opening of the poem is intended to establish. Everyone with a fair melodic repertoire in his head will be drawn to supply the unnamed melody. In my case it was undoubtedly the violin obbligato to the *Laudamus* in Bach's B Minor Mass, which in its bland serenity is the perfect musical counterpart of a slow and sinuous stream. Others may find this melody too warm and prefer to substitute something colder and more melancholy. It must be admitted, too, that in some performances the tempo is too brisk.

Another example of what might, in this instance, be called a 'reversed simile' appears in the first stanza of *Trees in the Moonlight*.

> Trees in the moonlight stand
> Still as a steeple,

And so quiet they seem like ghosts
Of country people— . . .

The first of these two similes is a comparison between things likely to be equally familiar: 'steeple' calls up the image of a church and so sets a tone of solemnity. 'Like ghosts of country people' is a different kind of comparison. Everyone knows what 'quiet' means, but few could claim to have seen 'ghosts of country people'. I have called this a 'reversed simile', because the familiar is likened to the unfamiliar. In fact, it is perhaps less a simile than a way of introducing the 'ghosts' which are the subject of the poem.

Vicary Square is an account of the houses in a square as they might appear to the eye of an observant and imaginative child. It is a sustained exercise in anthropomorphism, in which, by the use of metaphor, simile and personification, the houses around the square are given their separate individualities.

In Vicary Square at Tithe-on-Trent
The houses are all different,
As if they grew by accident.
For Number One
Is full of fun
With knob and knocker
To catch the sun;
And Number Four
Looks thin and poor,
And Number Five
Looks scarce alive,
And Number Seven, though clean and neat,
Looks like a lady without any feet.
But Number Eight
Is grand and great
With two fat lions
Beside the gate,
And Number Nine
Is deuced fine,
And Number Ten
Squats like a hen.

Number Twelve
Is by itself
Like a marble clock
Upon the shelf . . .

Then follows a number of houses described in less personal
terms, till:

Number Thirty
Is dark and dirty,
Number Forty
Is high and haughty,
Number Fifty
Is sly and shifty.
Fifty-Two
Has a door of blue,
Fifty-Three
Has a walnut-tree
And a balcony on the second floor
After Fifty-Four
There aren't any more.

Some houses, it will have been noticed, though different from
the others, are not personified.

A succession of similes and metaphors makes up *Fireworks*.

They rise like sudden fiery flowers
    That burst upon the night,
Then fall to earth in burning showers
    Of crimson, blue, and white.

Like buds too wonderful to name,
    Each miracle unfolds,
And catherine-wheels begin to flame
    Like whirling marigolds.

Rockets and Roman candles make
    An orchard of the sky,
Whence magic trees their petals shake
    Upon each gazing eye.

Since the subject of this poem is by its nature abstract—that is, not representational—it can only be rendered in terms of its similarity to natural objects—flowers, buds. To describe the night sky as a field crammed with brilliant flowers seemed to me the best way to convey the richness and brilliance of a firework display.

Seeds is reminiscent of the Anglo-Saxon riddles referred to earlier.

> A row of pearls
> Delicate green
> Cased in white velvet—
> The broad bean.
>
> Smallest of birds
> Winged and brown,
> Seed of the maple
> Flutters down.
>
> Cupped like an egg
> Without a yolk,
> Grows the acorn,
> Seed of the oak.
>
> Autumn the housewife
> Now unlocks
> Seeds of the poppy
> In their spice-box.
>
> Silver hair
> From an old man's crown
> Wind-stolen
> Is thistledown.

This is a series of five metaphors showing the appearance of the fruit of five different plants.

The Sea, quoted earlier, is a deliberate effort to explore the possibilities of metaphor in an attempt to find out how far there is a likeness between two quite dissimilar things. The inanimate sea is written of as if it were an animate creature, as if it had come to life in the shape of a giant shaggy dog. Here again is the first stanza:

> The sea is a hungry dog,
> Giant and grey.
> He rolls on the beach all day.
> With his clashing teeth and shaggy jaws
> Hour upon hour he gnaws
> The rumbling, tumbling stones,
> And 'Bones, bones, bones, bones'
> The giant sea-dog moans,
> Licking his greasy paws . . .

As I have said before, the instinct to animate the inanimate, either as a person or as a monster, is primitive. It runs right through Greek mythology and is exemplified in the conception of the monsters Scylla and Charybdis, the enemies of mariners in the *Odyssey*.

Alliteration is a basic feature of the English language in its simpler, more primitive aspects. It is not necessary to go back to Anglo-Saxon poetry to appreciate this. Many of our proverbial expressions are memorable because they are alliterative— 'wind and weather', 'hearth and home', 'bold as brass', to name only three of hundreds. The ear appreciates alliteration as a rhyme occurring at the beginning of a pair of words, just as it appreciates a full rhyme at the end. It is, therefore, a device to appeal to the child's mind and help to make him aware of the poetic and rhetorical qualities of language. The 'H' rhyme in *Ragged Robin* is an example of this kind of game with letters. 'H' is of course the principal letter used, but others occur, such as 'b' and 'w'.

> Heroes on horseback
> Hunt in their hundreds,
> Leaving their halls
> In the hurry of morn.
> High on the hilltop

Is heard the thunder
Of hooves, and the hue
Of hound and horn.

Here in their homesteads
Hover the housewives,
Baking and brewing
Or busy with brush.
Gaily they gossip
And stitch for the children;
For hunting and harrying
They care not a rush.

High in the heavens
The hooked moon hangs.
Home come the hunters
Hungry as hawks.
Never a hare
Has Harry the Huntsman
Caught the whole day,
But hark how he talks!

'Hunters on horseback
Are braggers and boasters!'
So say the housewives
Who give them their stew.
'Without us women
To work and wait on them
What would these heroes
Our husbands do?'

Alliteration occurs throughout poetry, and it is sometimes as difficult, and as necessary, to avoid it as to use it. I do not see how any rule can be drawn up. It is a matter of taste, of not overdoing a rather simple device. The lines quoted above, however, are a deliberate exercise in the device, as self-conscious as that of the Anglo-Saxon poets, though the rules of strict alliterative verse have been stretched.

In *Rain*, also from *Ragged Robin*, is found a blend of alliteration and onomatopoeia, the matching of sound to sense. No poet, no mere versifier worth anything, can fail to infuse his lines with some degree of onomatopoeia. The sound must echo the sense, if only because we do not use words that greatly violate their meaning by their sound. 'Sea', 'home', 'mountain'—all the common words sound like what they mean, if only because of association. Sound, as it were, spills over into meaning and becomes part of it.

> Rain and rain is all I see
> Falling on roof and stone and tree,
> And all I hear is rain and rain
> Hush-hushing on lawn and lane.
>
> Moor and meadow, fern and flower
> Drink the raindrops, hour by hour.
> How sparkling are the ivy leaves
> That catch the drops from farmhouse eaves.
>
> When in my attic bed I lie
> I hear it fall from the cloudy sky,
> Hush-hushing all around
> With its low and lulling sound . . .

Here the whole atmosphere suggests the soft, soporific effect of gentle rain falling straight out of the sky, not blown by any wind, as the listener lies in bed at night. The deliberately onomatopoeic compound 'hush-hushing' is reinforced by such combinations as 'lawn and lane', 'moor and meadow,' 'low and lulling'. The drowsy effect of the liquid sound 'l' and the labial 'm' was fully exploited by the arch-prosodist Tennyson and by others before him.

A similar example of onomatopoeia occurs in *Green Grass*, already quoted.

> Green grass is all I hear
> And grass is all I see
> When through tall fields I wander
> Swish-swishing to the knee . . .

Words such as 'hush and 'swish' are by their nature onomatopoeic formations. There are many such in the language, and
children respond to them and invent their own. *The Hippocrump*, a *Prefabulous Animile*, is more elaborately onomatopoeic,
appealing almost as much to the ear as to the eye.

> Along the valley of the Ump
> Gallops the fearful Hippocrump.
> His hide is leathery and thick;
> His eyelids open with a *Click*!
> His mouth he closes with a *Clack*!
> He has three humps upon his back;
> On each of these there grows a score
> Of horny spikes, and sometimes more.
> His hair is curly, thick and brown;
> Beneath his chin a beard hangs down.
> He has eight feet with hideous claws;
> His neck is long—and O his jaws!
> The boldest falters in his track
> To hear those hundred teeth go *Clack*!
>
> The Hippocrump is fierce indeed,
> But if he eats the baneful weed
> That grows beside the Purple Lake,
> His hundred teeth begin to ache.
> Then how the creature stamps and roars
> Along the Ump's resounding shores!
> The drowsy cattle faint with fright;
> The birds fall flat, the fish turn white.
> Even the rocks begin to shake;
> The children in their beds awake;
> The old ones quiver, quail and quake.
> 'Alas!' they cry. 'Make no mistake,
> It is *Himself*—he's got the Ache
> From eating by the Purple Lake!'
> Some say, 'It is *Old You-know-who*—
> He's in a rage: what *shall* we do?'
> 'Lock up the barns, protect the stores,
> Bring all the pigs and sheep indoors!'

They call upon their god, Agw-Ump
To save them from the Hippocrump.
'What's that I hear go hop-skip-jump?
He's coming! Stand aside there!' *Bump*!
Lump-lump!—'He's on the bridge now!'—*Lump*!
'I hear his tail'—*ker-flump, ker-flump*!
'I see the prickles on his hump!
It *is*, it IS—the Hippocrump!
Defend us now, O Great Agw-ump!' . . .

This contains not only such well-worn words as 'click' and 'clack', but also a more adventurous coinage, 'ker-flump', intended to give a precise sound-picture of something wet and heavy coming down on a resonant surface.

The literary device of personification is somewhat sophisticated for children, and I have used it only sparingly. 'King Frost' I have already mentioned. This is simple enough, since frost is an easily recognized phenomenon of physical nature. I will end by quoting a more demanding exercise in personification from *Ragged Robin*.

Of all creatures Quiet is the shyest;
She has her finger to her lips.
She loves not cities but a mountain lakeside
Where peaceful water laps.

At nesting-time to see the mother blackbird
Quiet on tiptoe creeps;
And in the kitchen with scarce a blink she watches
The mice come out for scraps.

In fairgrounds or by the August seaside
Quiet will not stop;
But walks in winter on snow fresh-fallen
With light and muffled step.

She loves the fireside when the guests have gone,
And downward the ember slips;
Beside the cot she lingers hardly breathing
Because the baby sleeps.

This is not a poem for the youngest reader. Not only is the abstract concept 'Quiet' personified as a shy girl; the rhyme-scheme is based entirely on assonance—'lips, laps', 'creeps, scraps' and so on. The assonances seemed to me to be suitable to the subject, for a full rhyme is more precise and, as it were, noisier than a half-rhyme. Although this is a poem for the more thoughtful reader, children, I repeat, do not need to consciously appreciate technical niceties. It is enough if they respond to the overall effect of a poem. But those—and there will be many—who want to go on to make poems of their own may enjoy an insight into how poems are made.

With this account of some of the devices used in poetry, especially simile and metaphor, I conclude what I have to say about writing poems for children. The important thing about technical devices is that they should not obtrude. If some of my poems have been consciously alliterative or onomatopoeic, that is because it can be amusing for children to be aware of such things as the sound-qualities of words and metrical and rhythmic forms. In other words, let an experiment sometimes be seen to be an experiment. After all, *musical* exercises, often published as 'Studies', have an honourable history.

As I conclude these pages, I see that my two fold exploration of the subject-matter and the form of poetry has been almost exclusively concerned with my own practice. I remarked at the outset that this is how it would be, I have written elsewhere in more general terms about poetry in education, and I have selected a number of anthologies of the work of widely differing poets. The subject-matter of my verse has been what interests me. It could not be otherwise. A friendly reviewer recently described my book *The Blackbird in the Lilac* as representing 'the mellifluous pastoral tradition'. Unfortunately he did not mention any other tradition or give examples of it. If by 'mellifluous' he meant that my poems sound all right, I take his comment as a compliment. If by 'pastoral' he meant that my poetic base is in the country, I cannot deny it: I have given reasons earlier why this had to be so. If there were any other 'tradition' in children's verse, I would be glad to know of it. The important thing, as I have said, is that children love variety, surprise, oddity. All that excites their imagination and their curiosity is the province of poetry.

As for the technique of writing, I have admitted to favouring a conservative view of form. This does not, of course, rule out experimentation. Whatever is seen to work, and felt to work, and heard to work is to be encouraged. Only, if it succeeds, it is no longer an experiment. Herrick and Hardy, to name only two, were among the most tireless of experimentalists in verse form: yet so sure was their touch, so resourceful their technique, so good their ear, that they are no longer regarded as experimental. They are taken to be conservative. I have no objection to unrhymed, a-metrical verse, provided it makes its own music and fulfils its own pattern. Too often there is no music and no pattern, and the ear is starved. But when the Arthur Waley or the Walt Whitman of children's *vers libre* appears, I shall salute him.

List of Quotations

POEMS BY THE AUTHOR QUOTED IN THE TEXT

Below is a list of all quotations in the text from books of verse by the author, as indicated in the following key.

WM *The Wandering Moon* (William Heinemann, 1950)
BL *The Blackbird in the Lilac* (Oxford University Press, 1952)
PA *Prefabulous Animiles* (William Heinemann, 1957)
RR *Ragged Robin* (William Heinemann, 1961)

If a poem is quoted in part only, this is indicated by ellipsis dots in the text; the title of the complete poem will be found below.

PART I

Chapter 1

> Age after age ('The Wandering Moon')   *WM*
> In the deep kingdom ('Under Ground')   *WM*
> Stocking and shirt ('Stocking and Shirt')   *WM*
> Hard as crystal ('Bells')   *WM*
> If pigs could fly ('If Pigs Could Fly')   *BL*
> The furry moth explores ('Explorers')   *BL*
> Gusty and chill ('Rum Lane')   *BL*
> Priam is the king of ashes ('Troy')   *BL*
> When I went down ('Kingdom Cove')   *BL*

Chapter 2

> In autumn down the beachwood path ('Beech Leaves')   *WM*
> I wish I were ('A Thought') *Teaching Poetry* (Heinemann
>   Educational Books, 1958)
> One day I built a castle ('The Castle')   *WM*
> On a stone chair ('The Statue')   *BL*
> There is a lady ('The Piano')   *BL*

Gently the river bore us ('Boating')   *BL*
The grasses nod together ('The Grasses')   *WM*
Lie on this green ('Village Sounds')   *WM*
Smooth and flat ('Stones by the Sea')   *WM*

Chapter 3

Sweet Miss Petal ('Miss Petal')   *WM*
Doctor John Hearty ('Doctor John Hearty')   *WM*
Poor Mrs Utter ('Mrs Utter')   *WM*
You push the door ('Miss Wing')   *BL*
In a huge hoary mansion ('Mr Bellairs')   *BL*
Pity poor Rumble ('Poor Rumble')   *BL*
Little Minnie Mystery ('Little Minnie Mystery')   *BL*
The people of Diddling ('Diddling')   *BL*
A scandalous man ('Mr Tom Narrow')   *WM*
Mr Kartoffel's a whimsical man ('Mr Kartoffel')   *WM*
Zachary Zed was the last man ('Zachary Zed')   *RR*

Chapter 4

Very very queer things ('Queer Things')   *WM*
The two old trees ('Mumbing Hill')   *WM*
Flowers are yellow ('Flowers and Frost')   *RR*
There was an old woman who sowed ('The Magic Seeds')
   BL
The King walked ('Three Singing Birds')   *BL*
Giant Thunder Striding home ('Giant Thunder')   *BL*
Mrs Farleigh-Fashion ('Mrs Farleigh-Fashion)   *WM*
Doctor Emmanuel Harrison-Hyde ('Doctor Emmanuel')
   WM

Chapter 5

Said Pluto the King ('Pluto and Proserpine')   *BL*
A stream far off ('The Moonlit Stream')   *BL*
Near Wookey Hole ('The Three Unlucky Men')   *BL*
The toadstool wood is dark ('The Toadstool Wood')   *BL*
Robin was a king of men ('Ragged Robin')   *RR*
Uncut is your corn ('Un-')   *RR*
There was an old wife ('The Old Wife and the Ghost')   *BL*
'I'm much fatigued' ('The Two Mice')   *BL*

Under the ground ('Rabbit and Lark')   *WM*
Mick my mongrel-O ('Mick')   *BL*
Along the valley of the Ump ('The Hippocrump')   *PA*
Through Dangley Woods ('The Doze')   *PA*
In mellowy orchards ('The Snitterjipe')   *PA*
'Up, up, my sons' ('The Blether')   *PA*
At Midsummer Fair ('Roundabout')   *WM*

Chapter 6

There was a man of Uriconium ('Uriconium')   *BL*
Through yonder park ('Yonder')   *RR*
Who will sing me the song of D? ('The Song of D')   *RR*
Jerusalem, Joppa, Jericho ('Jargon')   *RR*
Kay, Kay, ('Kay')   *RR*
I can get through a doorway ('The Wind')   *WM*
Hard and black is my home ('Fire')   *WM*
Two-boots in the forest walks ('The Intruder')   *BL*
I dance and dance ('Spells')   *WM*
Slowly the tide creeps up the sand ('Slowly')   *WM*
Shiny are the chestnut leaves ('Shiny')   *WM*
For a farthing and a penny ('A Farthing and a Penny')   *WM*
She sits by the sea ('A Mermaid Song')   *WM*
Run a little this way ('Run a Little')   *BL*
Mary, Mary, come and listen ('The Musical Box')   *WM*
Let no one suppose ('Let No One Suppose')   *PA*
Trees in the moonlight stand ('Trees in the Moonlight')   *BL*
Half the time they munch the grass ('Cows')   *BL*
The Old King of Dorchester ('The Ceremonial Band')   *BL*

PART II

Chapter 7

There met two mice at Scarborough ('Two Mice')   *BL*
O Harry, Harry! hold me close ('The Catipoce')   *PA*
A dappled horse stood ('The Grey Horse')   *WM*
Noah was an admiral ('Noah')   *RR*
That night I dreamed ('The Castle')   *WM*
Far from far ('Bobadil')   *BL*
In a blue, blue bonnet ('The Summer Party')   *WM*

In Avalon lies Arthur yonder ('Avalon') *RR*
When Pat plays his fiddle ('Pat's Fiddle') *BL*
I, with my mind's eye, see ('Islands') *RR*
Brand the blacksmith ('Brand') *RR*
This is the keep ('Kay') *RR*
I don't like the look of little Fan ('Little Fan') *WM*
The sea is a hungry dog ('The Sea') *WM*

Chapter 8

Age after age ('The Wandering Moon') *WM*
A dappled horse stood ('The Grey Horse') *WM*
Doctor John Hearty, though old ('Doctor John Hearty') *WM*
'Mother, oh mother!' ('Others') *WM*
Mick my mongrel-O ('Mick') *BL*
The King sent for his wise men all ('W') *BL*
The toadstool wood is dark ('The Toadstool Wood') *BL*
When Mrs Button, of a morning ('Mrs Button') *BL*
The moon is up ('Old Moll') *WM*
Little Minnie Mystery has packets ('Little Minnie Mystery')
     BL
In a huge hoary mansion ('Mr Bellairs') *BL*
Let no one suppose ('Let No One Suppose') *PA*
Oh, grim and gloomy ('Grim and Gloomy') *WM*
This is the superfluminous Osc ('The Osc') *PA*
Who went to sleep in the flower-bed? ('The Song of the
     Dumb Waiter') *WM*
Mrs Golightly's goloshes ('Mrs Golightly') *BL*
Grey is the sky ('Grey') *WM*
Waiting, waiting, waiting ('Waiting') *WM*
She sits by the sea ('A Mermaid Song') *WM*
The voice of magic melody ('My Singing Aunt') *BL*

Chapter 9

At sunset, when the night dews fall ('The Snail') *WM*
Shiny are the chestnut leaves ('Shiny') *WM*
About that kitchen neat and clean ('The Old Wife and the
     Ghost') *BL*
You'd say it was a wedding ('You'd say it was a wedding')
     WM

Downward the branching ('Under Ground')   *WM*
Mrs Farleigh-Fashion ('Mrs Farleigh-Fashion')   *WM*
A stream far off beneath the moon ('The Moonlit Stream')
    BL
Trees in the moonlight stand ('Trees in the Moonlight') *BL*
In Vicary Square ('Vicary Square')   *WM*
They rise like sudden fiery flowers ('Fireworks')   *BL*
A row of pearls ('Seeds')   *BL*
The sea is a hungry dog ('The Sea')   *WM*
Heroes on horseback ('Heroes on Horseback')   *RR*
Rain and rain is all I see ('Rain')   *RR*
Green grass is all I hear ('Green Grass')   *RR*
Along the Valley of the Ump ('The Hippocrump')   *PA*
Of all creatures Quiet ('Quiet')   *RR*